Why is Norway Outside the European Union?

European University Studies
Europäische Hochschulschriften
Publications Universitaires Européennes

**Series XXXI
Political Science**

Reihe XXXI Série XXXI
Politikwissenschaft
Sciences politiques

Vol./Bd. 605

PETER LANG
Frankfurt am Main · Berlin · Bern · Bruxelles · New York · Oxford · Wien

Gamze Tanıl

Why is Norway Outside the European Union?

Norwegian National Identity
and the Question
of European Integration

PETER LANG
Internationaler Verlag der Wissenschaften

Bibliographic Information published by the Deutsche Nationalbibliothek
The Deutsche Nationalbibliothek lists this publication in the Deutsche Nationalbibliografie; detailed bibliographic data is available in the internet at http://dnb.d-nb.de.

© The Munch Museum / The Munch-Ellingsen Group / BONO, Oslo 2011

ISSN 0721-3654
ISBN 978-3-631-60778-7
© Peter Lang GmbH
Internationaler Verlag der Wissenschaften
Frankfurt am Main 2012
All rights reserved.

All parts of this publication are protected by copyright. Any utilisation outside the strict limits of the copyright law, without the permission of the publisher, is forbidden and liable to prosecution. This applies in particular to reproductions, translations, microfilming, and storage and processing in electronic retrieval systems.

www.peterlang.de

Foreword

For a comparatively small states situated on the northern periphery of Europe, Norway has attracted a notable number of scholars interested in understanding its complex, yet close relationship with the evolving European Community/Union (EC/EU). Not least there have been notable studies that have sought to utilize identity-based and other explanations for why this Nordic state has applied and then rejected full EC/EU membership terms. Yet, many of these have not sought to unpack how Norwegian identity – or as Tanil refers to it – 'identification' – influence the Norwegian people's attitudes towards European integration for those outside the Nordic region – something that remains essential if cross-national comparative lessons are to be drawn now and in the future. This new work by Gamze Tanil provides a useful introduction for those (especially non-Nordic) interested parties that may not have an immediate understanding of the nuances of the characteristics of Norwegian identity.

Through her usage of identification approaches, combined with an extensive presentation of the specific features of Norwegian nation-building, Dr Tanil offers a well-written and lucid account of how Norway's history and culture shape the prism through which many Norwegians view the merits of their country's relations with the emerging European Union.

Professor Lee Miles
Department of Political Science
Karlstad University, Sweden

Table of Contents

Foreword 5

Preface 9

Acknowledgements 11

Chapter 1: Introduction 13
1 Research Area 13
2 Research Subject 14
3 Theoretical Background 18
4 Methodology 20
5 Research Structure 21
6 Relevance of this Research 22

Chapter 2: Theoretical Background 23
1 Introduction 23
2 Theories of Nationalism 23
3 National Identity Dynamic and Foreign Policy 28
4 Theoretical Hypotheses 32

Chapter 3: The Construction of the Norwegian National Identity 35
1 Introduction 35
2 Construction of the Norwegian National Identity 37
    2.1. History 37
    2.2. Foundational Myth 43
    2.3. Territorial Bond or Homeland 46
    2.4. Idea of Norwegian People 48
    2.5. Invented Traditions 50
        National Political Institution 50
        National Language 52
        National Flag 54
        National Anthem 55
        National Day 57
        National Hero 58

3 Role of the National Art and Literature in the Construction and
   Institutionalization of the Norwegian National Identity 59
   3.1. Art 60
   3.2. Music 63
   3.3. Literature 65
4 Conclusive Remarks 66

Chapter 4: The Functioning of the Norwegian National Identity Dynamic ... 71
1 Introduction 71
2 1961-62: The First Application to EEC and the First Debate 72
3 1967: The Second Attempt to Get Norway into the EC 75
4 1972 Debate on EC Membership 76
   4.1. Application Discussions 76
   4.2. Membership Negotiations 76
   4.3. Referendum Campaigns 77
       Actors 78
       Arguments 78
       Result 82
   4.4. Conclusive Remarks 82
5 1992 EEA Agreement and the Period of Adaptation 84
6 1994 Debate on EU Membership 85
   6.1. Application Discussions 85
   6.2. Membership Negotiations 86
   6.3. Referendum Campaigns 89
       Actors 89
       Arguments 91
       Result 111
   6.4. Conclusive Remarks 112

Chapter 5: Conclusion 117

Chapter 6: Bibliography 125

Preface

This book analyzes Norwegians' conception of the European Union membership as a product of ideas and identity regarding themselves and the European Union. In this way, it offers a way of combining two different areas of study, namely identity politics and international relations, and examines the impact of the domestic structure, which is defined as a combination of identities and interests, on the foreign policy formulations. By doing so, it seeks to fill the gap in the existing literature on the subject, which has in general emphasized the economic aspects of the relations between nation-states and the European Union. It also contributes to the mainstream international relations theory which has for so long ignored the role of identity politics in the international system.

This book employs 'national identity' not only to describe the condition in which a mass of people have made the same identification with national symbols, but also to refer to the possible mass mobilization of this people to act as one psychological group when there is a threat to, or the possibility of enhancement of, these symbols of the national identity. The 'national identity dynamic' that in the formulation of foreign policies definition of the 'self' as oppose to 'other', perception of 'threat' and people's mass mobilization against the perceived or actual threat to protect their self definition/national identity are crucial elements. This perspective contributes well to the analysis of the Eurosceptic nations, and helps avoiding reductionist approaches which conceptualize national interest as a function of material conceptions of power.

Asst. Prof. Dr. Gamze Tanil
Department Chair, International Relations
Istanbul Arel University

Acknowledgements

This book would not have been possible without the financial support and critical encouragement of a large number of people. This manuscript has been a long time in the making and I have benefited enormously from different institutions. To start with, the University of Oslo ARENA Centre for European Studies provided valuable research atmosphere at the initial stage of this research in 2002; and Professor John Erik Fossum highly contributed by his useful comments on the early stages of this research. The University of Liverpool generously funded my research visits to Norway which contributed to my understanding of the subject. I am extremely grateful for the support, patience, and critical encouragement of Professor Lee Miles who read and discussed the entire manuscript several times. I would also wish to thank Karlstad University Department of Political Science for their providing valuable insights and discussions at the final stage of the process. I have benefited enormously from many presentations and discussions with Associate Professor Hans Lödén and Associate Professor Curt Räftegård, Dean of the Faculty of Social and Life Sciences. Finally, I would like to thank Istanbul Arel University for funding the publication of this book. While it would be impossible to thank each and every one individually, I would like to extend my special thanks to my family and friends for their never ending support.

Chapter 1: Introduction

1. Research Area – A Social Laboratory

'The small nations that comprise the Scandinavian area constitute a social laboratory for the Western world.'
Walter Galenson, *Labour in Norway* (1949)

'It is the 'rooftop of the world'. Once the home of ruthless Vikings, now it is a haven of peace; once isolated off the routes of travel by land and sea, now on main air traffic lanes; once poor, now productive and prosperous beyond the average; barbarous late into European history, now an admired pattern of enlightened society. This is Scandinavia, Norden, the North'.
Franklin Daniel Scott, *Scandinavia* (1980)

Most political scientists are engaged with the politics of big powers such as American, British, and Russian politics: Nordic countries attract little interest since they are not great powers, nor are key players in the international arena. But the pearl is hidden in the shell. When examined closely it is recognized that the small and sparsely populated Nordic countries punch beyond their weight due to their enviable political and economic characteristics. First of all, they symbolize for most people 'the countries, which stand for peace, disarmament, and cooperation in the international arena' (Wæver 1992:77). Secondly, they provide lessons to other countries with their 'mature parliamentary democracy, competitive market economy, comprehensive welfare provisions, social and environmental standards, tradition of open democratic government, internationalism, and a shared preference for a free trade global economy' (Miles 1996:7). For these reasons, researchers and scholars of Nordic politics describe the region as a 'social laboratory'.

One salient aspect in this social laboratory is Norway's rejection of the European Union membership twice in the recent history. This policy choice is important in two respects: For more than fifty years the European political arena has been dominated by the enthusiastic regional integration attempts, and almost all European countries, except for a few, have become members of this regional union. In such an international environment, Norway's turning down the membership option is of significance. No other country, except Greenland which left the Union after a national referendum in 1982, has actually rejected membership. Secondly, Norway rejected the EU membership not only once but twice in

20-year period notwithstanding the changing domestic and international environment. The continuity of negative public attitude towards the European Union should be explained only with solid reasons and structural factors.

Norway's position as a 'willingly outsider' attracts attention of many scholars, and there's already a large amount of scholarly work on the subject[1]. This study differs from the previous work in that it takes a different route by employing 'social constructivist approach' together with 'national identity dynamic' in explaining this policy choice. I believe that the introduction of a psychological approach to the study of identity politics, which is not very common, is very interesting, and contributes well to the existing literature.

Existing literature on the subject is dominated by the Nordic scholars who extensively researched and wrote on the Norwegian rejection of EC/EU membership. As a result, it has become a very well known academic field among the Nordic audience. However, both the subject area, i.e. Nordic politics, and the policy choice of Norway, i.e. rejection of EU-membership, are quite virgin fields in other national contexts. This research provides a reflective and introductory work by a non-Nordic scholar for the non-Nordic audience. To be precise, this text is especially written for the non-Norwegian audience with an aim to introduce Norwegian case to non-Norwegians.

To summarize, this research aims to provide a new perspective to Norway's relations with the EU, and to introduce Norwegian European policy to the non-Norwegian scholarship and audience. With these two distinctive aims it contributes to the analysis and understanding of the Norwegian European policy.

2. Research Subject – A Way to the North[2]

Since its first manifestation as the European Coal and Steel Community following the signing of the Treaty of Paris on 18 April 1951 with six Member States – West Germany, France, Italy, the Netherlands, Belgium, and Luxembourg- the European Union (EU) have proceeded much becoming a unique international entity that directly affects the daily lives of over 500 million citizens today. However, there are some countries which have been reluctant to join this union.

Having been dominated by Danes for 400 years and by Swedes for 90 years until its independence in 1905, Norway has stayed at distance from both the prob-

---

1   See Andersen 2000; Archer 2005; Archer and Sogner 1998; Beate and Listhaug 1995; Bjørklund 1996,1997; Egeberg 2005; Gestöhl 2002; Ingebritsen 1995,1998; Matlary 1993; Rokkan 1966; Saglie 2000; Saeter 1996.
2   The name of the country, 'Norway' means 'a way to the north'.

lems and the enthusiastic integration attempts in Europe. Luckily, Norway was outside of the terrible military and economic conflicts which were dominating Europe at that period. It had a comparatively lower military tension and comparatively favourable economic situation. Jørgen Løvland, the first Norwegian Minister of Foreign Affairs after Norway's independence from Sweden in 1905, stated his prime task as 'to keep Norway out the combinations and alliances that can drag the country into belligerent adventures together with any of the European warrior states' (quoted in Sverdrup 2000:84). So, the European integration attempts, basis of which is rooted in the desire of the French to keep German military power under control, had barely any relevance for Norway. Besides, occupation by Germany during the Second World War also bred the suspicion against the continental European countries. Main policy was not to involve in the war-making games of the big European countries.

The application of the close partner, Britain, followed by the close Scandinavian neighbour, Denmark, to the EC in 1967 caused a turning point in this foreign policy towards Europe. However, for a country which has a tradition of corporatist pluralism, making such a big decision was not that easy. The decision was not to be taken only by the state and government officials, but instead, it would be a collective decision with the contribution of all parts of the nation. After long and heated debates and campaigns on the issue, Norwegian citizens turned down the EC-membership option in a referendum in September 1972 with a 'No' majority of 53.5%.

Time for the second attempt came with the applications for full EU membership of the countries Austria, Sweden and Finland between 1989 and 1992. Although 57% of the Finish voters, 66,6% of the Austrian voters, and 52% of the Swedish voters favoured the EU membership, on 28 November 1994 52.2% of those voting in the Norwegian referendum on EU membership rejected once more the government's proposal that Norway should join the EU and, implicitly, the terms negotiated for membership. With this second case, deep reservations among Norwegian citizens against the EU membership became clear.

The explanations for this foreign policy choice vary widely among scholars. A sizeable but scattered number of contributions by electoral researchers building on the work of Stein Rokkan try to demonstrate how historical cross-cutting cleavages[3], dormant in everyday Norwegian politics, have been activated to produce a winning majority for the no-side. Certain roles such as those of city-dweller or country-dweller, producer or consumer are supposed to inculcate

---

3 Stein Rokkan and Henry Valen's model consists of two main axes: the territorial-cultural dimension (centre-periphery), which is related to the national revolution, and the economic-functional dimension (producers and consumers; employers and employees), which is associated with the industrial revolution (Rokkan 1967; Valen 1981).

in individuals certain interests, and because of these interests they are supposed to vote in a certain way. While this explanation is able to pinpoint the pattern of behaviour, it does not shed light on the question of motivation.

The negative connotation of 'union' is employed to explain Norwegian public's foreign policy choice: Tamnes and Egeberg argue that 'there was an enduring, underlying broad scepticism towards becoming part of a 'union' once more' (Tamnes 1997). It seems to them as if both the union with Denmark (1380-1814) and the union with Sweden (1814-1905) were still present in a negative way in the collective memory of the Norwegian people (Egeberg 2003:6). These arguments are supported by those who claim that usually not the nature but the form of cooperation matters for Norway: 'Norway's relationship to the EU fits a historical pattern, when it comes to forms of international cooperation. This pattern, which is characterised as 'nationalistic internationalism', has two elements: (1) In principle, Norway is for all kinds of international cooperation, but (2) the form of such cooperation is often problematic' (Andersen 2000:2). Therefore, it is argued that 'participation is reluctant and a central concern is to find special institutional arrangements and special solutions' (Lundestad 1985:45). However, this explanation is also insufficient to explain the underlying motivations.

Seeking to provide 'the most obvious explanation for EU-opposition' in Norway, Bjørklund confines his analysis to 'economic self-interests' of various social groups: 'Norwegian farmers, who are described as the world's most subsidized and perceive their business interests at stake; Norwegian fishermen, seeking protection of fishing resources from the fleets of EU countries; and the Norwegian public sector, characterized by a protected economy and afraid of the threat of cuts in public sector funding due to harmonization of the Norwegian to a common EU standard' were against the Norwegian EU-membership (Bjørklund 1997:145; Bjørklund 1996:29-30). Similarly, 'political economy based sectoral approach' of Ingebritsen focuses on the role of the leading sector (petroleum) and secondary sectors (agriculture and fisheries), and their political representation and influence on the country's elite which exert pressure on the decision over EU membership. According to her, 'the capacity of the state to pursue an integrationist strategy varied according to the political influence of leading sectors' (Ingebritsen 1998:33).

However, economic self-interest based analysis is not enough to explain Norwegian voters' persistent policy choice on EU-membership. First of all, such sectoral approaches almost seem to suggest that the political leaders of the country are the pawns of the leading sectors and play only a marginal role in the decision on EU membership. Secondly, only a small and shrinking percentage of Norwegians are involved in the primary economic sectors of fishery and agriculture. Instead of such economic self-interest based approaches, this research asserts that an analysis of foreign policy choices does not imply an analysis of material facts only, but also the human interpretation (social construction) of these material conditions in any national context.

A more encompassing approach moves beyond rationalist premises and takes account of the identity politics. Iver Neumann tries to explain Norway's choice of staying outside the EU by analysing how the agriculture and fisheries sectors as well as others arguing in favour of a 'no' were able to 'capture the heart of the nation', and thus ensure that 'people with only the most flimsy material ties to these sectors nonetheless voted 'no' to EU membership in 1972 and 1994 referenda' (Neumann 2002:89). With such an approach, he perceives the naysayers 'not as aggregations of individual rational interests, but as instantiations of identity politics' (ibid:89).

Identity politics is also of great importance for Ole Wæver who argues that an analysis of domestic discourses regarding 'we' concepts, like state, nation, and Europe in major European states can explain their foreign policy choices. For him, in most cases, 'the question of European integration turns out to be the question of how the different state/nations in different ways have 'Europe' integrated into their 'we's' (Wæver 2002:25). His analysis is thus focused 'not simply on 'who' we are, but on the way(s) one conceives this 'we' through the articulation of different layers of identity in complex constellations of competition and mutual definition' (ibid:25). In his analysis there are three levels of constructions at the national context: (1) basic construction of the state/national identity, (2) construction of 'Europe' vis-à-vis the state/national identity, (3) construction of concrete policy for Europe, meaning that a specific European policy (level 3) involves a construction of a particular Europe (level 2) building upon a construction of the state-nation constellation (level 1).

Indeed, the perception of the EU as 'a threat to core Norwegian values, national traditions and state sovereignty' (Ingebritsen and Larson 1997:215) stood out as the first and foremost in both 1972 and 1994 EU-referendum debates in Norway. Kristen Nygaard, in a lecture at a conference in 1995, after mentioning the negative implications of the EU-membership on Norwegian natural resources, agriculture, fisheries, environment, justice and home affairs, economy, democracy and sovereignty, concluded that 'these aspects relate to very fundamental characteristics of Norwegian society, characteristics of which we pride ourselves and which we want to be strongly present in Norway also in the future' (Nygaard 1995:10).

Based on this background, this research analyzes Norwegians' conception of the European Union membership as a product of the ideas and identity with regards to themselves and the European Union.

At this point, it is important to clarify that this study is concerned with the perception of Norwegian people of themselves and of the EU, and their perception of interests and threats associated with the EU-membership. This study is not concerned with the actual facts about the EU, i.e. what the European supranational identity actually is, what effects it has on the national identities, whether it is really a threat to national systems; rather it solely focuses on the Norwegian people's perceptions and ideas about themselves and the EU. Such an analysis is significant both for demonstrating a different, and contrasting, perspective of the European Union and for understanding the reasons leading to this contrasting perception.

3. Theoretical Background

Regarding the major cultural and political identifications in Europe today, one of the most significant outgrowths of the European economic and political integration has been the heated debate concerning the future of the nation-state and the ideology of nationalism. While the functions and symbols of sovereign nation-states have received increased attention, the plans to centralize more political power in Brussels have received increased antagonism. Many fear that the strengthening of the Union's power would cause the member states to lose not only much of their independent legislative force, i.e. their independence as sovereign states, but also many of their socio-political and cultural peculiarities, i.e. their national identities.

As outlined in the previous section, issues of identity and ideas about self and other were significant and decisive in Norwegians' perception of the EU-membership. EU-membership was seen as a threat to the core values of Norwegianness, and the Norwegian way of life. By joining the EU, it was argued by the anti-EU campaign, 'Norway would enter into a union with others who did not speak Norwegian, were not acquainted with the uniqueness of Norway's connection to the countryside and traditional values, nor would they be likely to conform to the 'norsk hver dag'' (Ingebritsen and Larson 1997:216). The romantic identification with rural traditions and nature was in sharp contrast to a more urbanized European society.

It is important to underline that in this debate, what is referred to as 'Norwegianness' is not an objective, qualifiable picture of what it means to be Norwegian, but rather, it is what Hobsbawn and Anderson have identified as 'invented traditions' and 'imagined communities' respectively (Hobsbawn 1983, Anderson 1991). Hobsbawm's 'invented traditions' means 'a set of practices, normally governed by overtly or tacitly accepted rules and of a ritual or symbolic nature, which seek to inculcate certain values and norms of behaviour by repetition, which automatically implies continuity with the past' (Hobsbawn and Ranger 1983:1). Anderson's 'imagined political community' is imagined because 'the members of even the smallest nation will never know most of their fellow-members, meet them, or even hear of them, yet in the minds of each lives the image of their communion' (Anderson 1991:6-7). These images and ideas about Self and Other are so significant in people's minds that they can easily influence important foreign policy choices. As Ingebritsen points out, if these romanticized images were not shared by a large number of Norwegians, the political manipulation of such images and ideas would not only be pointless, it would be unlikely to figure prominently in such an important national debate (Ingebritsen 1998:126). Relying on the images of Norwegian ideas and traditions, leaders of the anti-EU political coalition represented the EU as an undesirable, unnecessary compromise.

If we are to accept the effect of the national identity on the interest formation, then we should clarify the source and the formation of that identity, which is able to impact on the foreign policy of the state. So, first of all, the concept of *identification* should be analyzed: What is identity and identification, and why do individuals need identification? Bloom's answer to this question is that 'in order to achieve psychological security, every individual possesses an inherent drive to internalize –to identify with- the behaviour, mores and attitudes of significant figures in his/her social environment; i.e. people actively seek identity' (Bloom 1990:23). Once an identification has been made, the process is not over, rather, individuals try to enhance and to protect the identifications they have made. This inherent drive to enhance and protect the existing identifications influences the perception of the individual of his/her surrounding environment.

Among all other collective identities –family, territory, social class, religion, ethnic, and gender-, *national identity* provides the most cohesive and potent base for collective identification and mobilization. The definition of the national identity is provided by Smith as 'a named human population sharing an historic territory, common myths and historical memories, a mass, public culture, a common economy and common legal rights and duties for all members' (Smith 1991:14). Therefore, national identity describes the condition in which 'a mass of people have made the same identification with the features of the nation', which are listed as 'an historic territory, or homeland; common myths and historical memories; a common, mass public culture; common legal rights and duties for all members; a common economy with territorial mobility for members' (ibid:14).

The *power* of the national identity lies in its ability to produce both political integration and national mobilization. This can be best explained by the phrase 'national identity dynamic'. *National identity dynamic* describes 'the potential for action which resides in a mass which shares the same national identification' (Bloom 1990:53): 'If a mass of people exists whose individual constituents share the same national identification, then this mass may act as one unit in situations which affect the shared identity. They may act together to make new identifications, or they may act together to enhance and protect identifications already made' (ibid:53).

It is argued in this research that national identity describes (1) the condition in which a mass of people have made the same identification with national symbols –have internalized the symbols of the nation-, and (2) the possible mass mobilization of this people to act as one psychological group when there is a threat to, or the possibility of enhancement of, these symbols of national identity.

This point underlines the basic approach to be taken in the analysis of Norwegian rejection of the European Union membership. The perception of the self and the other, the perception of threat, and people's mass mobilization to protect their self definition against the perceived threat will be discussed in line with this theoretical background throughout this study.

4. Methodology

This research employs a qualitative research because it gives a deeper comprehension of the problem under study and enables the researcher to apprehend the problem in its entirety. Sources of qualitative data can be primary, i.e. observation, interview and questionnaire, and/or secondary, i.e. official documents, reports, public and official records, and essays.

In search for empirical data for the presentation and validation of the role of national identity on the Norwegians' perception of themselves and the EU, and on their rejection of the EU-membership, this research employs both primary and secondary sources of data: *The primary sources* include observations and conversations carried out among academics, experts, and senior researchers in Norway in order to reach at general information on ideas and perceptions on the Norwegian identity and its role on the foreign policy choices. *The secondary sources* include: (1) literature on nationalism, national identity, Norwegian history and national identity, and the EU-debates in Norway; (2) government reports, official papers, and speeches on Norway's EU-policy; (3) basic programs, posters, strategic papers, newspapers of the EU-opponents which describe what and why they are against integration; (4) description and presentation of the 'Norwegianness' in art, literature, travel guides, souvenir shops, talks; (5) statistical data about the voting behaviour of the Norwegian electorate.

5. Research Structure

This book is divided into five chapters:

Chapter 2 presents the theoretical framework. It introduces theories of the nations, nationalism, national identity, national identity dynamic, and the discussion of the impact of the national identity on the foreign policy decisions. It also presents how these theories are applied to the research area.

Chapter 3 analyzes the construction of the Norwegian national identity. It starts with the analysis of the composing features of the Norwegian national identity, i.e. history, foundational myth, idea of a Norwegian people, and invented traditions. In this analysis, Norwegian art and literature (music, painting, literature, and theatre) are referred to as useful and popular mechanisms enabling the internalization and institutionalization of each of these elements. Construction of Europe as the 'other' is also added to this analysis. Finally, formalization of the national identity through symbols, ceremonies, and customs are mentioned.

Chapter 4 analyzes the functioning of the Norwegian national identity dynamic in its relation with the European integration process mainly in 1972 and 1994. The chapter is divided into four sections: (1) 1961-62 debate over membership to the European Community; (2) 1967 debate over membership to the European Community; (3) 1972 debate over membership to the European Community; and (4) 1994 debate over membership to the European Union. In each of these sections, Norwegian citizens' perception of themselves and the European Union, public discourses and arguments of both yes- and no-sides, and the perceived threats of the EU-membership to the national values and identity are presented and discussed. The aim of this chapter is to analyze how national identity functions in the making of foreign policy decisions.

Chapter 5 presents the conclusions of this study. In particular, the domestic elements that shaped the preference structure of the people and politicians of Norway on the EU-membership issue are examined; and responses are given to the questions of 'how influential can the national identity dynamic be in the making of foreign policy decisions', and 'how can such an argument offer an alternative to the mainstream international relations theories'.

6. Relevance of This Research

This research is relevant for at least four reasons:

First of all, theories of political integration have mainly examined integration processes 'from the centre', and not from the position of those who are (or are not) to be integrated. By analyzing a non-EU member country, i.e. Norway, this study sheds light on the perception of the EU from outside, and on the problems and debates that the EU-membership initiates in a national context.

Secondly, Norway may be a small country that has little influence on its international environment, but this does not mean that it has no choice in its external policies. Certainly, prosperous economy had a big role in enabling Norwegian citizens to make such a comfortable choice[4], but whatever the reasons are, Norway as a small country demonstrated that small countries have also 'power' to decide. This research is important for showing the power of a small state.

Third, Norwegian case demonstrated very idealistically that the most important decisions at the state level are not subject to the will of 'statesmen', but instead, they are going to be taken with reference to the feelings of the people. This case should be appreciated since it symbolizes the solidarity in the society and the democracy in its most idealistic form.

Finally, its relevance lies in its contribution to the social constructivist theory. Most social constructivist scholars are criticized for that 'they fail to provide concrete and testable causal mechanisms through which the process of choosing policies and defining interests takes place, with the ultimate goal of saying something about which ideas and discourses influence which policies under which circumstances' (Moravcsik 1999:671). This research aims to fill that gap between the identity definitions and the foreign policy decisions by bringing the 'national identity dynamic' into the picture.

---

4   Ingebritsen and Larson argue that 'only in oil-dependent Norway did we see societal interests thumbing their nose at Europe and having the luxury of hanging on to traditional notions of state sovereignty' (Ingebritsen and Larson 1997:219).

Chapter 2: Theoretical Background

1. Introduction

Nations have been one of the defining features of the recent history, and a major actor of social and political life for almost two centuries. They form the foundation of our social consciousness, the cognitive framework of our perception of reality. They play such a crucial role in our lives that large numbers of people are prepared to make great personal sacrifices –up to and including life itself- in the struggles needed to achieve or defend the political sovereignty of their nation. What's more, contemporary trends in world politics demonstrate that the significance of nations and nationalism has not been withered away; rather, it is very likely that they will continue to be relevant for us in the foreseeable future. In order to understand why national identities shape our lives so crucially, sources and functions of national identities need to be clarified.

The aim of this chapter is to explain, discuss, and compare the theories on nations, national identities, and national identity dynamic. This discussion is relevant in order to later explain how Norwegian national identity is formed and how it functioned in the case of EU-membership debates. A clear understanding of the formation and functioning of the national identity is crucial for the analysis of the national identity dynamic in the Norwegian context in the following chapters.

2. Theories of Nationalism

Nation is defined by Smith as 'a named human population sharing an historic territory, common myths and historical memories, a mass, public culture, a common economy, and common legal rights and duties for all members' (Smith 1991:14). The nation is different from the state in that 'while the state refers exclusively to public institutions, differentiated from, and autonomous of, other social institutions and exercising a monopoly of coercion and extraction within a given territory, the nation signifies a cultural and political bound, uniting in a single political community all who share an historic culture and homeland' (ibid:14).

Although there are many different ways of approaching to the concept of 'nation', there is an agreement on the fact that nations are not born, rather they are created. Gellner's famous definition states that 'nations are not natural, God-given phenomena; rather there is another force which engenders nations, that is nationalism' (Gellner 1983:56). Similarly, Calhoun argues that it is the 'nationalist way of thinking and speaking which helps to make nations' (Calhoun 1997:99). Conceptualization of nations not as natural phenomena, but as products of nationalism leads researchers to seek for the ways and means of this production.

With an aim to shed light on the ways and means of the production of nations, *modernist approach* finds the essence of nations and nationalism in the modern processes like capitalism, industrialism, emergence of the bureaucratic state, urbanization, and secularism. There are two different interpretations of these processes: John Breuilly, Paul Brass, Eric Hobsbawn emphasize the role of politics and power struggles in the emergence of nations, while Ernest Gellner, Benedict Anderson and Miroslaw Hroch give priority to social/ cultural factors in the emergence of nations.

Hobsbawn conceptualizes both nations and nationalism as products of 'social engineering'. For him, what deserves particular attention in this process is the concept of 'invented traditions' by which he means 'a set of practices, normally governed by overtly or tacitly accepted rules and of a ritual or symbolic nature, which seek to inculcate certain values and norms of behaviour by repetition, which automatically implies continuity with the past' (Hobsbawn and Ranger 1983:1). These traditions are invented by ruling elites who felt threatened by the incursion of the masses into politics.

For Hobsbawn, the period from 1870 to 1914 can be considered as the apogee of invented traditions. He mentions three major innovations of the period as particularly relevant: 'the development of primary education; the invention of public ceremonies; and the mass production of public monuments' (ibid:270). As a result of these processes, 'nationalism became a substitute for social cohesion through a national church, a royal family or other cohesive traditions, or collective group self-presentations, a new secular religion' (ibid:303). Therefore, the role of nations was established as 'securing the obedience and loyalty of their subjects, now redefined as citizens, in an age when other forms of legitimacy like religion or dynasty were rapidly losing ground. By establishing continuity with a suitable historical past, they smoothed the transition to a new kind of society' (ibid:303).

From a different perspective, *Gellner* finds the essence of nations and nationalism in the transition from agrarian society to the industrial one: 'Reformation produced the literacy and scripturalism, individualism, links with mobile urban populations; and industrial division of labour produced the population explosion, rapid urbanization, labour migration, economic and political penetration of previously more or less inward-turned communities. In order to meet the demands of industrial societies, i.e. universal literacy and a high level of numerical, technical and general sophistication, a large educational system was created. There was a need for some organism to ensure that this literate and unified culture was being effectively produced, and that the educational product was not sub-standard, and it was only the state which could do this. Therefore, the imperative of exo-socialization, the production and reproduction of men outside the local intimate unit, was the main clue to why state and culture must be linked' (ibid:38).

Therefore, he argues, 'nations as a natural, God-given way of classifying men, as an inherent though long-delayed political destiny, are a myth; nationalism, which sometimes takes pre-existing cultures and turns them into nations, sometimes invents them, and often obliterates pre-existing cultures: that is a reality and in general an inescapable one' (Gellner 1983:49). For him, it is the need of modern societies for cultural homogeneity that created nationalism, and nationalism is sociologically rooted in modernity; it is a product of the transition from 'agro-literate' societies, regulated by structure, to industrial societies, integrated by culture.

Anderson focuses on the cultural roots of nationalism. For him, in Western Europe the 18th century marks the dusk of older cultural conceptions on men's minds, and this provided the historical and geographical space necessary for the rise of nations: 'The very possibility of imagining the nation only arose historically when and where there was (1) the fade of the idea that a particular script-language offered privileged access to ontological truth; (2) a gradual decline of religious community and dynastic realm; (3) and a change in the apprehensions of time' (Anderson 1991:36). With the slow, uneven decline of these interlinked certainties, first in Western Europe, later elsewhere, under the impact of economic change, he explains, social and scientific discoveries and the development of increasingly rapid communications took place and changed the cultural conceptions: 'No surprise then that the search was on for a new way of linking fraternity, power and time meaningfully together. Nothing perhaps more precipitated this search, nor made it more fruitful, than print-capitalism, which made it possible for rapidly growing numbers of people to think about themselves, and to relate themselves to others, in profoundly new ways' (ibid:36).

Thus, he regards the modern nation as an artefact, 'an imagined political community' developed and spread through rapid communications: 'The nation is imagined because the members of even the smallest nation will never know most of their fellow-members, meet them, or even hear of them, yet in the minds of each lives the image of their communion. Ultimately, it's this fraternity that makes it possible for so many millions of people willingly to die' (ibid:6-7).

This brief presentation of modernist approaches to nationalism signifies the role of political and socio-cultural factors that lead to the emergence of nations and nationalism. While these factors open the way for the emergence of nations, the construction of nations is finalised by the 'discursive practices'. It is argued by Stuart Hall and Ruth Wodak that the national identity is constructed in discourse.

Wodak argues that 'if a nation is an imagined community and at the same time a mental construct, an imaginary complex of ideas containing at least the defining elements of collective unity and equality, of boundaries and autonomy, then this image is real to the extent that one is convinced of it, believes in it, and identifies with it emotionally. The question of how this imaginary community reaches the minds of those who are convinced of it is easy to answer: it is constructed and conveyed in discourse, predominantly in narratives of national culture. National identity is thus the product of discourse' (Wodak et al. 1999:22).

Hall's definition of national identity is also based on the national discourse: 'National identities are not things we are born with, but are formed and transformed within and in relation to representation. We only know what it is to be 'English' because of the way 'Englishness' has come to be represented, as a set of meanings, by English national culture. So, a nation is not a political entity but something which produces meanings –a system of cultural representation. People are not only legal citizens of a nation; they participate in the idea of the nation as represented in its national culture. A nation is a symbolic community' (Hall 1992:292).

For him, national culture as a discourse has power to generate a sense of identity and allegiance: 'national culture is a way of constructing meanings which influences and organizes both our actions and our conception of ourselves' (ibid:293). He argues that 'national cultures construct identities by producing meanings about 'the nation' with which we can identify; these are contained in the stories which are told about it, memories which connect its present with its past, and images which are constructed of it' (ibid:293).

The argument that the core of the national identity is 'invented traditions' or 'constructed national culture' may meet with two challenges: First of all, the fact that national cultures are constructed based upon national narratives, i.e. stories, memories, and images, may give way to challenge their reality. It should be noted that national narrations do not arise out of nothing; they are brought forth, reproduced and disseminated by actors in concrete institutional settings. In other words, they are based on actual historical memories, stories, symbols, and their usage in institutional contexts creates an emotional bond among those who come to share them. Indeed, 'the fact that nationality is a story does not challenge its reality, because myths are not mystifications' (Ram, cited in Wodak et al. 1999:23). The second challenge might be that if the nation is an imagined community, how does this imaginary community reach the minds of those who are convinced of it, believes in it and identifies with it emotionally? The answer is that there are certain representational strategies that are employed to construct our commonsense views of national belonging or identity. Hall argues that a narration of national culture contains five fundamental aspects:

1- First, there is the *narrative of nation*, as it is told and retold in national histories, literatures, the media and popular culture. These provide 'a set of stories, images, landscapes, scenarios, historical events, national symbols and rituals which stand for, or represent, the shared experiences, sorrows, and triumphs and disasters which give meaning to the nation'. As members of an imagined community, we come to share this narrative because 'it lends significance and importance to our monotonous existence, connecting our everyday lives with a national destiny that pre-existed us and will outlive us' (Hall 1992:293).
2- Second, there is the *emphasis on origins, continuity, tradition, and timelessness*. National identity is represented in narratives of national culture as the original identity which is present in the nature of things but sometimes lies dormant and has to be awakened from this slumber. By this way, the image of national character is presented as unchanging, unbroken and uniform.
3- The third discursive strategy is what Hobsbawn and Ranger call the *invention of tradition*: 'Traditions which appear or claim to be old are often quite recent in origin and sometimes invented. 'Invented tradition' means a set of practices ... of a ritual or symbolic nature which seek to inculcate certain values and norms of behaviours by repetition which automatically implies continuity with a suitable historical past' (Hobsbawn and Ranger 1983:1).
4- The fourth strategy is to devise a *foundational myth:* It is 'a story which locates the origin of the nation, the people, and their national character so early that they are lost in the mists of, not 'real', but 'mythic' time' (Hall 1992:295). Such myths play a role both in the officially sanctioned narrations of existing nations, and in the antithetical narratives which are used as instruments to find new nations.
5- The final strategy is to symbolically ground the national identity on the idea of a *pure, original people or 'folk'*. However, in the realities of national development it is rarely this primordial folk who persist or exercise power. Gellner points out that 'when the Ruritanians donned folk costume and trekked over the hills composing poems in the forest clearings, they did not also dream of one day becoming powerful bureaucrats, ambassadors and ministers' (Gellner 1983:61).

Therefore, discourse of national culture serves two purposes: First, 'it constructs identities which are ambiguously placed between past and future, and it straddles the temptation to return to former glories and the drive to go forwards ever deeper into modernity' (Hall 1992:295). Second, it creates an 'impulse to unify':

'However different its members may be in terms of class, gender or race, a national culture seeks to unify them into one cultural identity, to represent them all as belonging to the same great national family' (ibid:296).

In addition to the discursive elements of the national identity, the contribution of state –or more specifically its administrators and officials- to the generation of national identities is described by Bourdieu as follows: 'Through classificational systems inscribed in law, through bureaucratic procedures, educational structures and social rituals, the state moulds mental structures and imposes common principles of vision and division. It thereby contributes to the construction of what is commonly designated as national identity' (Bourdieu 1994:7). In other words, 'the state shapes those forms of perception, of categorisation, of interpretation, and of memory which serve as the basis for a more or less immediate orchestration of the habitus which forms the basis for a kind of national common sense, through the school and the educational system' (Wodak et al. 1999:29).

This section outlined some of the important and influential perspectives of the nationalist literature. The conclusion is that employing political or socio-cultural factors to explain the construction of nations and national identities is not enough, rather a more insightful perspective is needed to explain how nations and national identities reach the minds of those who are convinced of it, believes in it and identifies with it. The approach which can help the researchers to understand and explain this process is the discursive construction of the national identity. To summarise, 'the national identity of individuals who perceive themselves as belonging to a national collectivity is manifested in their social practices, one of which is discursive practice. The respective national identity is shaped by state, political, institutional, media and everyday social practices, and the material and social conditions which emerge as their results, to which the individual is subjected. The discursive practice as a special form of social practice plays a central part both in the formation and in the expression of national identity' (ibid:30). Following section seeks to describe and understand the impact of national identity on foreign policy choices.

3. National Identity Dynamic and Foreign Policy

Many social constructivist scholars deal with the impact of national identities and interests on foreign policy choices[5]. The contribution of this research to the existing social constructivist literature is that it includes the individual psychology into the analysis by employing Bloom's 'national identity dynam-

---

5   See Marcussen et al. 1999, 2001; Marcussen 2005

ic'. This approach offers a useful insight to questions such as: 'Why do large groups of people act together in certain political situations?', 'How do masses mobilize for or against certain foreign policy decisions?', 'Is there a method for explicating the relationship between the mass attitudes and actual foreign policy decisions?'

To start with, Bloom argues that 'in order to achieve psychological security, every individual possesses an inherent drive to internalize –to identify with- the behaviour, mores and attitudes of significant figures in his/her social environment; i.e. people actively seek identity' (Bloom 1990:23); and that 'through a shared identification, individuals are linked within the same psychological syndrome and will act together to preserve, defend and enhance their common identity' (ibid:26).

The *identification theory* of Bloom follows as such (ibid:50):

1. Identification –the mechanism of internalizing the attitudes, mores and behaviour of significant others- is a psycho-biological imperative based in the earliest infantile need to survive.
2. Identification is a dynamic adaptive mechanism as much at work in adults as in infants.
3. A satisfactory synthesis of identifications, or identity stability, is crucial for a sense of psychological security and well-being. Identity enhancement leads to a greater sense of well-being; identity diffusion leads to anxiety and breakdown.
4. As life circumstances change, individuals may make new and appropriate identifications. Individuals may also seek to protect and enhance identifications already made.
5. Insomuch as a group of individuals shares a common identification, there is the potential for that group to act together to enhance and protect that shared identity.

In today's complex society, although individuals have 'multiple identities as gender, space/territory, social class, religion, ethnic, and nationality' (Smith 1991:4), among all those collective identifications, nationality or national identity proves to be the most dominant one being the most cohesive and potent base for collective identification and mobilization. How this evocation of a mass shared identification happens is obviously a crucial issue for political integration and nation-building within a state.

Bloom talks about *nation-building* process referring to both 'the formation and establishment of the new state itself as a political entity', and 'the processes of creating viable degrees of unity, adaptation, achievement, and a sense of national identity among the people' (Bloom 1990:55). To achieve the latter, he argues, the individual should experience the state, and this experience should evoke identification. This internalization and identification can be realised only if symbols of the state present an appropriate attitude in situations of perceived threat, or symbols of the state behave beneficently towards the individual (ibid:61). These symbols of the state can be formal individuals, institutions and ideas, e.g. monarchs, structured benefit systems and constitutions, or informal individuals, institutions and ideas, e.g. tavern patriots, longbows and ballads as long as the symbol is clearly associated with the state. In addition to these symbols, formal and informal social rituals ensure people communicate together about the commonly held identification[6] (ibid:62).

When nation-building is achieved, continues Bloom, identification links the individual citizen with his or her fellow citizens through the shared national identity: 'If there has been a general identification made with the nation, then there is a behavioural tendency among the individuals who made this identification and who make up the mass national public to defend and to enhance the shared national identity' (ibid:79). Therefore, *national identity* describes not only the condition in which a mass of people have made the same identification with national symbols –have internalized the symbols of the nation-, but also the possible mass mobilization of this people to act as one psychological group when there is a threat to, or the possibility of enhancement of, these symbols of national identity (ibid:52). So, the 'power' of the national identity lies in its ability to produce both political integration and national mobilization.

National identity dynamic explains the relationship between the national identity, the mass national public, government foreign policy decisions, and the international environment. Bloom argues that if images and experiences concerning international events are presented to the mass public in such a way that either national identity is perceived to be threatened, or the opportunity is present to enhance national identity, then the identification imperative will tend to work through the mass public as a national whole. In such situations, the mass national public will act as one group to secure, protect and enhance their national identity. The national identity dynamic, therefore, describes the social-psychological dynamic by which a mass national public may be mobilized in relation to its international environment. This, claims Bloom, is to state explicitly that the mass national public has a clear and psychologically coherent relationship with international affairs: 'The mass national public will mobilize when it perceives either that national identity is threatened, or that there is the opportunity of enhancing national identity' (ibid:79).

---

6 This is similar to Hobsbawn's invented traditions which are defined as a set of practices of a ritual or symbolic nature, which seek to inculcate certain values and norms of behaviour by repetition (Hobsbawn and Ranger 1983:1)

National identity dynamic, therefore, provides a theoretical tool for explicating the complex relationship between the national identity, the mass national public, government foreign policy decisions, and the international environment. The logic of this relationship is as follows (ibid:80):

1. Images of the international environment can mobilize the national identity dynamic,
2. Government may create/manipulate these images in order to mobilize the national identity dynamic,
3. Factors beyond government control may create/manipulate these images. The mobilized national identity dynamic may then affect government foreign policy-making.

The mass national public is thus shown to be a discrete actor in the foreign policy decision-making process (ibid:80):

1. The mass national public will always react against policies that can be perceived to be a threat to national identity,
2. The mass national public will always react favourably to policies which protect or enhance national identity.

To summarize, the influence of the national identity dynamic on foreign policy making is outlined by Bloom as follows (ibid:132):

1. The mass national public will mobilize if it perceives that there is a threat to, or the opportunity of enhancing, national identity.
2. The mobilization of the mass national public is, by definition, the largest possible mobilization within a nation-state.
3. It is a feature of domestic politics that there be competition to appropriate the national identity dynamic.
4. The national identity dynamic, if mobilized, necessarily influences government decisions.

The identification theory of Bloom explains how the mass national public –via a shared identification- is evoked into being, and then explains how that mass national public may tend to behave. Therefore, the profound usefulness of this theory lies in its ability to explain both political integration and national mobilization (ibid:129).

4. Theoretical Hypotheses

Based on this theoretical background, this research takes the 'identity politics' route, specifically the 'national identity dynamic' approach, together with the 'middle-ground social constructivist' approach in the tripartite analysis of the national identity, mass national public, and the government's foreign policy choices.

This research accepts and employs five main theoretical assumptions:

I. National identities are not things we are born with, but are formed and transformed within and in relation to representation. National cultures construct identities by producing meanings about 'the nation' with which we can identify; these are contained in the stories which are told about it, memories which connect its present with its past, and images which are constructed of it (Hall 1992:292-293).

II. National identity is constructed by means of 5 elements: (1) narrative of nation as a set of stories, images, landscapes, scenarios, historical events, national symbols and rituals which stand for, or represent, the shared experiences, sorrows, and triumphs and disasters which give meaning to the nation; (2) emphasis on the common homeland or territory signifying the origins, continuity, tradition, and timelessness; (3) the invention of traditions as Hobsbawm and Ranger call, i.e. the invention of a set of practices, of a ritual or symbolic nature which seek to inculcate certain values and norms of behaviours by repetition which automatically implies continuity with a suitable historical past; (4) the foundational myth which is a story which locates the origin of the nation, the people and their national character so early that they are lost in the mists of, not real, but mythic time; (5) the idea of a pure, original people or 'folk'.

III. The construction of the national identity takes place through classificational systems inscribed in law, through bureaucratic procedures, educational structures and social rituals, by means of which the state moulds mental structures and imposes common principles of vision and division, and thereby contributes to the construction of what is commonly designated as national identity (Bourdieu 1994:7).

IV. The power of the national identity lies in its ability to produce both political integration and national mobilization. National identity describes not only the condition in which a mass of people have made the same identification with national symbols –have internalized the symbols of the nation-, but also the possible mass mobilization of this people to act as one psychological group when there is a threat to, or the possibility of enhancement of, the symbols of national identity (Bloom 1990:52).

V. An analysis of foreign policy choices does not imply an analysis of material facts only, but also the human interpretation (social construction) of these material conditions in any national context. In other words, this research takes the 'identity politics' route in the analysis of foreign policy choices.

The following chapters try to illustrate and empirically validate these main theoretical assumptions by analyzing the construction and the functioning of the national identity in Norway.

CHAPTER 3: The Construction of the Norwegian National Identity

'Nordic identity is about being better than Europe.'
Ole Waever (1992:77)

'If this is your land, where are your stories?'
Aboriginal proverb (Chamberlin 2004:13)

1. Introduction

It is argued in this research that national identity describes (1) the condition in which a mass of people have made the same identification with national symbols –have internalized the symbols of the nation-, and (2) the possible mass mobilization of this people to act as one psychological group when there is a threat to, or the possibility of enhancement of, these symbols of national identity. Chapter 3 analyzes the first part of this theoretical assumption, and Chapter 4 analyzes the second part.

Regarding the 'construction' of the national identity, it is argued that this construction is carried out by the intelligentsia by using 5 elements:

(1) History (narrative of nation as a set of stories, images, landscapes, scenarios, historical events, national symbols and rituals which stand for, or represent, the shared experiences, sorrows, triumphs and disasters which give meaning to the nation): The struggle for independence from compulsory unions with Denmark and later Sweden for 400 years; and later the World War II, German occupation and resistance will be dealt with in this context.

(2) The foundational myth (a story which locates the origin of the nation, the people and their national character): The Vikings, their virtues and triumphs will be dealt with in this context.

(3) The territorial bond or 'homeland': This aspect is not about where the nation state's border is, but about the linguistic and symbolic description and 'construction' of the national territory or homeland.

(4) The idea of a pure, original people or 'folk': The construction of the idea of the Norwegian people as opposed to the foreign-influenced civil servant stratum, and the pure Norwegian way of life or 'norsk hver dag' will be mentioned and analyzed in this context.

(5) Invented traditions (the invention of a set of practices, of a ritual or symbolic nature which seek to inculcate certain values and norms of behaviours by repetition which automatically implies continuity with a suitable historical past): Construction of the national political institutions which represent and defend 'the people' rather than 'the state', construction of the national language by returning back to the 'roots', construction of the national symbols such as national flag, national anthem, national day, and national hero, will be dealt with in this context.

In this analysis, Norwegian art and literature (music, painting, literature, and theatre) will also be referred to as useful and popular mechanisms enabling the construction and internalization of each of these elements.

The main period of analysis here is the 'long 19th century', which constitutes 'the making of the Norwegian nation' (Neumann 2002:94). Following the 1814 Constitution started a new era which signalled a moral-spiritual necessity to (re)constitute the Norwegian nation and the self-identity of the Norwegians. In the words of Ivar Aasen, it was the time 'to legislate, to sanction, to act, to approve, to establish the norms and values which will give shape to that identity which Norway, Norwegian and the Norwegian had always had despite the dark period of alienation and non-jurisdiction' (quoted in Burgess 1999:80). The elements of 'Norwegianness' needed to be redefined and accentuated as the basic composing elements of the new nation-state. Therefore, a clear understanding of this 'construction' is necessary in order to understand Norway's later encounters with Europe.

To summarize, this chapter focuses on the analysis of the Norwegian nation-building process, and the 'construction' of the fundamental elements of Norwegian national identity. It is important to underline a few important points here:

1) First of all, the aim of this section is not an analysis of the Norwegian nation-state building, or simply state-building; rather it is specifically the 'nation-building' process carried out by the intelligentsia, artists, and politicians starting from the 19th century[7]. However, when necessary the state-building process will also be dealt with in order to shed light on these twin processes, although it is not the main concern of this research.
2) Secondly, broad and embedded themes across elite and public constructions of national identity are analysed with an aim to shed light on later instances of the same broad themes that constrain Norwegian EU-debate. Such an analysis

---

7   Hobsbawn maintains that these are two separate concepts: invention or construction of the nation is defined as the construction of a collective identity or community through a shared ethnic, linguistic or cultural heritage, and that of the nation state is defined as the construction of a political unit with precise territorial boundaries (Hobsbawn 1997:105).

is important to detect the long-term stable trends about the internalization and functioning of the national identity in the Norwegian context.
3) Third, in the Norwegian context, it can be argued that the establishment of the nation-state reinforced the nationhood which was already deep-seated among public. Therefore, the notion of 'nation' existed in Norway even before the establishment of the Norwegian nation-state. Employing such a perception, the elements of this notion of 'nation' are analysed as the 'constructing' elements of the national identity of the later established Norwegian nation-state.
4) Finally, the approach employed in this research is the thick constructivist approach rather than the thin one (while the former tries to explore the myths associated with identity formation, the latter threats identities as possible causes of action). Employing a thick constructivist approach, this research tries to explore the myths associated with the construction of the elements of the Norwegian national identity rather than solely surfacing their functions.

2. Construction of the Norwegian National Identity

2.1. History

The grand narrative of Norwegian national history can be summarised as 'the foundation of the medieval kingdom; its decline and the Danish period; the background to self-determination and of the free constitution of 1814; the constitutional and national struggles leading to the independence in 1905; and the sovereign nation-state afterwards (Simensen 2000:93).

Medieval Norway developed as a mature state under Haakon IV (1217-63) and his son Magnus the Lawmender. During this period, the power of the monarchy increased ending in victory both over the Church and the nobles, and the traditional secular aristocracy was replaced by a serving aristocracy. However, towards the end of the period, the state revenues were scarcely adequate to finance any expansion of the administration apparatus of the Crown and the State (Dagre 1996).

The beginning of the end for independent Norway came when the country became dependent for its grain imports on the Hanseatic merchants who gradually took over control of Norwegian trade. Then in the middle of the 14th century the great plague known as the Black Death struck Norway and killed off half its population of 350,000. Norway was already the weakest and most vulnerable of the northern nations but now the plague wiped out 240 of its 300 noble families (Connery 1966:221).

Norway gradually passed under Danish control, first as a member of the Union of Kalmar under Queen Margrete of Denmark in the 1380s. However, the last stroke came on October 30, 1536 the date which marked the end of Norway as an independent kingdom. The national assembly in Copenhagen decided that Norway was to be subservient to the Danish Crown, like any other Danish possession. Norway's Council of the Realm was disbanded, and the Norwegian church lost its autonomy (Dagre 1996). As Jespersen puts it, 'the locus of sovereignty moved from estate meetings to the crown of Denmark, represented by King and Council' (quoted in Neumann 2002:91). Danish became the official, ecclesiastical and school language, and Danes swarmed into Norway to exploit its resources.

In the Napoleonic Wars, Norway, as an appendage of Denmark, found itself involved in the war on France's side. At the Battle of Leipzig in 1813 Napoleon suffered heavy defeat. One of his opponents on the battlefield, Sweden, had previously lost Finland to the Russians, and now wished to have Norway as a safeguard on its western border. Sweden's allies had therefore pledged Norway to it as one of the spoils of war. In the Peace of Kiel of January 1814 the Danish King handed Norway over to his Swedish opponents. In this way ended 434 years of union between Norway and Denmark (Dagre 1996).

At that time, state administration was in the hands of the civil servants stratum (*embedsmenn*) who formed the core of the ruling class. In the midst of the transfer of Norway from Denmark to Sweden, they started to organise and orchestrate a political campaign with an aim to make Norway a country on a par first and foremost with Denmark and Sweden, a process that requires Norway to differentiate itself from its neighbours on all grounds.

Christian Frederik, the heir to the Danish-Norwegian throne, was serving as viceroy in Norway at the time of the decision to give Norway to Sweden. His ambitions coincided with the plans of Norwegian political elite to declare Norway independent of foreign rule. Both agree that the first thing to do was to organise a meeting of representatives of the Norwegian people – not only civil servants but also peasants. So, citizens gathered in their churches on Sundays to vote for their representatives, and the congregations took an oath that they would 'defend Norway's independence and sacrifice life and blood for their beloved native country' (Midgaard 1963:69).

The elected representatives met at Eidsvoll, forty miles north of Oslo, in April 1814. The meeting lasted five weeks and produced a constitution on 17th of May, and Christian Frederik was elected unanimously as the king. With the signing of the Eidsvoll Constitution, Norway declared its own rights of freedom and independence for the first time since the end of the Late Middle Ages. However, the Swedes objected to these revolutionary moves; the eighteen-day war, fought between the Swedes and the Norwegians, resulted in a peace treaty which both sides agreed that the Eidsvoll Constitution would remain in force, but Christian Frederik had to abdicate and the Swedish king would be recognized as the ruler of the union of Sweden and Norway. Norway would remain its own country, free to manage its own affairs, with its own national assembly and taxation rights.

Although not enough to produce a sovereign Norwegian state yet, the Eidsvoll Constitution can either be conceptualized as a natural consequence of a Norwegian national consciousness which had been developing for some time[8], or as the very origin of the Norwegian sentiments, and the birth of politico-cultural thought of the Norwegians as such. In both cases, the year 1814 was 'Norway's annus mirabilis, when, a flame of feelings melded older identity elements into a new patriotism' (Neumann 2000:240).

In fact, the use of Norwegian history for the Norwegian nation building started even before 1814. Gerhard Schøning, a historian, writing in 1781, made it his task to convince Norwegians that they had a common and proud history which flowered particularly in the High Middle Ages[9]. Later, Henrich Steffens lectured to Norwegian students on romanticism in Christiania in 1802-3 and thus planted the philosophical seeds. Nicolai Wergeland, a minister, writing against Danish rule, argued that the 400 years of Danish rule had suppressed and usurped Norway and Norwegians, and focused on Norwegian history with the goal of branding Danish culture as foreign to Norway (Neumann 2002:95). In the 1830s, first a society then a journal devoted to the study of Norwegian history was formed with an interest in the language and history of the Norwegian people (ibid:95). Wergeland's son, Henrik, postulated Norwegian history as falling into two parts or two 'half rings': the Viking age and the period after 1814. The Danish period which lay between these two half rings was no more than a bad piece of welding for historians to remove (ibid:95). In the years 1858-1865 Ernst Sars wrote a coherent history of Norway during the association with Denmark, trying to show that Norwegian society had a distinct character and a development quite different from the Danish during those centuries (Fulsås 2000:243).

The most important national result of Norwegian 19th century historical research was 'the postulation of a separate and subaltern Norwegian subject, with a culture different from the Danish one' (Neumann 2002:95). The Norwegian culture, which had survived in the nooks and crannies of Norwegian valleys and

---

8   Fulsås (2000:244) conceptualizes it as "the result of a development deeply rooted in the 'people's' own history".
9   See Gerhard Schøning (1781) Norges Riiges Historie

fjords, had to be resuscitated. The aim was to 'awake the sleeping nation to a new life by historians, activists and other political activists' (Neumann 2000:243). Therefore, the history of the country became the subject of a careful research. Eminent historians[10] wrote scholarly works on medieval Norway, and reedited and commented on the Old Norse literature. The need for a grand historical narrative to buttress the self-confidence of the new nation was obvious, and the patriotic motivation of the first professional historians to satisfy this need was explicit. The task was to show that the Norwegian people were one of the oldest and historically most renowned in Europe, and not just a weak product of contemporary fermentations (Simensen 2000:91). To achieve this end, a grand image of the old Norse kingdom was constructed, largely build on the rich Saga material (ibid:91). The hidden literary treasures from the 'dark centuries' (folk tales, legends and ballads) were re-discovered and published. The proud history of the nation was strongly emphasized and nationalized. In this way, 'the conception of history presented a continuity of understanding, a principle of national will, and of the realisation of 'national destiny" (Burgess 1999:86).

The sequence of events towards the achievement of full independence began in December 1898 when the Norwegian parliament voted to remove the Union symbol from the flag of the Norwegian merchant marine. Assembling at Karlstad, the two sides were described as 'like one rock against other' (quoted in Derry 1973:168), but a sensible compromise emerged eventually. With the referendum on independence in 1905 Norway emerged as a fully sovereign state.

To summarize, Norway in the 19th century faced the task of both state-building and nation-building after having been ruled by the Danish for 400 years, and experienced an imposed political union with Sweden for nearly a century. Norwegian national identity was constructed in the 19th century against Danish cultural residue with an aim to establish Norwegian 'state' against the union, Norwegian 'language' against Danish, and Norwegian 'people' against Danish-influenced civil servant stratum. A return to the untouched, pure language and culture of the countryside, and to the glorious successes and virtues of the Vikings was eminent in this process.

The disastrous events of the 20th century consolidated the 'other' element in the Norwegian national identity –this time against the warrior states of Europe.

When the Second World War broke out in 1939, Norway, along with its Scandinavian neighbours, declared itself neutral. However, to make use of the Norwegian territory and coastline, particularly because airfields and submarine bases in Norway would be of great help in the battle against Britain, Hitler invaded Norway on April 9, 1940.

---

10 Rudolf Keyser (1803-1864); Peter Andreas Munch (1810-1893); Ernst Sars (1835-1917); Halvdan Koht (1873-1965).

Although Denmark, attacked the same day, succumbed almost immediately, Norway proved to be a tougher nut to crack, despite its unpreparedness. Shortly after the first attack, the members of the Government came together and ordered mobilisation; and the state of war was declared. Meanwhile, German warships forcing their way up to the Oslo fjord encountered with a quick and magnificent resistance from a small navy force. Owing to their opening fire on the German cruiser and sinking it, the Germans lost nearly two thousand men, including a key Gestapo force and the administrators who had been assigned to organise occupied Norway. Thus, the several hours delay before the German fleet could reach Oslo enabled the King and the royal family, the government, almost all members of the Storting, the gold reserves of the Bank of Norway (twenty-three truckloads of gold worth 240 million kroner), and secret papers to make their getaway. The King and the Government established a government-in-exile in England in order to carry on the struggle for Norway's freedom (Dagre 1996).

A Norwegian army was established and a Norwegian air force and navy were built up, and these fought with distinction in the war. The Norwegian merchant marine of 25,000 men and more than a thousand ships also fought in the war at the cost of 4000 seamen's lives and about half the fleet was sunk. Besides, an underground army, supplied and directed from London, was organised, and some of these troops were trained as sabotage groups, function of which was to destroy vital industrial and military installations.

Meanwhile, 'the people' of Norway did not remain silent. In the occupied portions of Norway people refused to cooperate with their new leaders. Thousands of Norwegian *civil servants, teachers, judges, clergymen and others* who refused to serve the occupiers were imprisoned or made to work in the mines. But this did not break the general resistance. *Teacher and student resistance* at the University of Oslo forced the closing of the University; and the Rector of the University and several hundred students were arrested and sent to Germany as prisoners. *The bishops* conducted strongly worded campaigns in their pastoral letters against the principles and practices of the 'new era', as a result of which they were forced to move from their parishes. The attempt to mobilise *Norwegian youth* for labour corps to work for the Germans under the name of 'national labour service' was not successful; thousands of Norwegian boys hid in the mountains and forests rather than be enrolled in the national labour service. The Nazis tried to get all sports organisations under their control, but met with a united front. *Sportsmen and athletes* refused to take part in public competitions. *Norwegian newspapers*, when compelled to print German propaganda material, would use as many German words as possible to alert their readers. Besides, *secret newspapers* circulated in large numbers and brought news from the war outside and the struggle in Norway.

All open resistance was forbidden by the new authorities, but this did not destroy the will to resist among the Norwegian people; and splendid solidarity and comradeship were displayed by the people of Norway. In this resistance the use of national symbols is significant for its presenting the functioning of the national identity dynamic. The first example is the usage of *paper clips*. Paper clip is significant as a national symbol for being a Norwegian invention, and representing solidarity (since it is used for keeping things together). When the Germans ordered Norwegian men to stop wearing flowers in their lapels on patriotic occasions, particularly the birthday of their exiled King, the men started wearing paper clips instead. Due to the implications of this symbol, it became a sign of resistance. The second example is the usage of *red stocking caps*. The stocking cap is also a Norwegian invention, and also it reminds of communism. They were used so wide-spread among Norwegian people as a means of protesting the occupation forces that the troubled Germans had to pass a law to prohibit people wearing those caps unless it is less than -6 C°. However, Norwegians did just the opposite. They wore that cap when it is more than -6 C°, but didn't wear it when it is less than -6 C°. These two cases demonstrate very well how the Norwegian people resorted to the symbols of the national identity in case of a threat to its existence.

Professor James A. Storing wrote that: 'This was certainly an interesting period for the student of national psychology, since most of the so-called Norwegian traits were dramatically exposed during the occupation years. Subtle obstructionism, dogged individualistic enterprise, stubborn resistance to the invasion of privacy, disregard for personal safety, and a passionate love of country, both as a geographic and a spiritual entity, all came out in sharp relief' (quoted in Connery 1966:229).

Storing's argument is significant for the goals of this research. He draws attention to the national psychology and functioning of the national identity dynamic against a perceived threat. At such times, as it is exemplified very well by the Norwegian resistance to the German occupation, the elements and symbols of the national identity (for example, paper clips and red stocking caps) came to the front and exposed bravely and proudly against the 'other'. This usage of national symbols against the perceived or actual threat is a good example of the national identity dynamic.

With the unconditional surrender of the German Army, King Haakon, after an absence of five years, returned to Norway on June 7, 1945.

The war years taught three lessons:

1) Together with the events of 1814 and 1905, 1945 was the third instance of liberation from powerful European states (first Denmark, then Sweden, and finally Germany). This situation reinforced the fear of 'union' which has nega-

tive connotations for the Norwegian people reminding of the memories of the 1814, 1905, and 1945.
2) Since no European country came to the aid of Norwegians during the occupation, the events of 1940-45 reinforced the link to NATO rather than Europe (later become the EC/EU).
3) Although Norwegians perceive themselves as liberated their country from German occupation by 'defending Norway's independence and sacrificing life and blood for their beloved native country', the reality is that the German troops left due to their surrender to the allied forces. Thus, the 1945 liberation can be seen more as a part of the 'construction of a glorious history' than a reality.

To summarise, the making of Norwegian history consists of three parts: (1) a glorious medieval past; (2) decay, loss of independence, and long union with Denmark (1380-1814); (3) independence in the 19th century. The task of Norwegian historians and nation-builders was to establish continuity in Norwegian history, whereby the state of the 19th century would appear as the legitimate heir to the medieval kingdom. The solution was to resort to the democracy and independence lay hidden in the freedom of the peasant class of the Middle Ages who were the carriers of historical continuity (Simensen 2000:92). With this aim, the Norwegian culture (folk tales, legends and ballads) which had survived in the nooks and crannies of Norwegian valleys and fjords were re-discovered and published. A reference to the free Norwegian peasant and the Storting as the main carrier of the independence had been frequently made.

Therefore, a distinct Norwegian national identity was constructed on three elements: (1) Norwegian 'state' against the union; (2) Norwegian 'language' against Danish; (3) Norwegian 'people' against Danish-influenced civil servant stratum. The construction of the 'self' against the 'other' was completed; later the 'other' was to be redefined as the Swedish (during union with Sweden), the German (during Nazi occupation), and the European (during debates on EC/EU-membership).

2.2. The Foundational Myth

The Vikings, who were described by their contemporaries as 'brutal and bloody', have become objects of uncritical admiration because of their 'adventurous spirit and gifts of improvisation'. From the 9th century to the 11th, they figured prominently in the history of Western Europe as raiders, conquerors and colonists. This section aims at shedding light on how and why the Vikings were used as the foundational myth for the Norwegian national identity.

The period known as the Viking Age was the time of the Viking movement overseas, when Viking ships sailed from Scandinavia, at the heart of the Viking world, out across the northern hemisphere, on voyages of piracy and invasion, and journeys of commerce, exploration and settlement (Graham-Campbell 2001:10). Among the major causes of the Viking raids, there was 'the expansion of European commerce and the development of new trade routes, which made privacy attractive, rewarding and inevitable for people who lacked the luxuries of wealthier and more fortunate lands' (Connery 1966:217). Out of nowhere the 'Northmen' burst on to a comparatively stable European society to shake its complacency: 'they colonized new lands, traded over seemingly impossible distances, fought bravely and with spirit, and established themselves ultimately in a series of nation-states. Their medieval descendants recorded some of the Viking deeds in a romanticized form in stories that belong with the great literature of the world –the Norse sagas' (Graham-Campbell 2001:1). The sagas talk about the achievements of Viking warriors and merchants, their gods (which mirror their people's personality and lifestyle), and their ships (which are the most easily and widely understandable symbol of the Vikings).

To start with, the Vikings were described as 'tall, blond figures possessed with a raging fury which they release upon other countries'[11], 'young and fight-seeking men, who are extremely skilled as sailors and warriors'[12], 'destructive, young warrior-seamen who sailed out of the fjords of the northern European peninsulas' (Logan 1992:17); and the Viking civilization as 'vibrant, untamed, and raw, which had a strong and unmistakable impact on much of the rest of Europe and on lands across seas and oceans' (ibid:16).

Brøndsted describes the Vikings as 'proud, adventurous, with a yearning for glory, a desire to excel in battle, and a scorn for death. These qualities of heroism and virility, combined with their mercantile skills, made them a powerful and dangerous race. Early monastic historians, in their records of the Vikings, emphasized the cunning, cruelty, and treachery of this warlike people. The sagas, on the other hand, show them in a different light; telling of the boldness, generosity, frankness, and self-discipline of these famous warriors. No doubt in the aggregate they possessed all the qualities, complimentary and otherwise, which were ascribed to them: the Vikings were not all alike. But one thing they did have in common: a daring resoluteness that made their period the greatest in the history of the North' (quoted in Connery 1966:217).

Having great courage, strength and guile as well as violence and passion at the time of war was something to be exalted; and inheriting all these characteristics was something to be proud of for the Norwegian people. These characteristics

---

11 See http://www.luth.se/luth/present/sweden/ history
12 ibid.

were believed to have enabled them to live in the wild nature, and to survive by working very hard in the difficult geographic and climate conditions. At the time of constructing a national identity, the proud, adventurous, glorious, heroic, generous Vikings were a precious foundational myth to resort.

The Viking gods, like the individuals who created them, were violent, ardent and passionate. They displayed the virile qualities the Vikings valued so much – brutality, anger, lust, humour- as well as their virtues – courage, strength and guile (Cohat 1992:106). Cohat describes the pantheon of Viking gods as such: 'Three main gods, Thor, Odin and Frey, each with his own symbol, are marvellous heroic figures of Scandinavian imagination, and mythical ancestors of their race. Odin is the god who dominates all others. He is the god of knowledge and of war or, more precisely, of victory. The god of the aristocrats, Odin, carries a spear. Thor is the son of Odin. Almost human in character, violent but benevolent, he is the most popular god with the common people and peasants. He protects the world of men from giants, little forest sprites, from cold and from hunger. The thundering god of the peasants, Thor carries a hammer. Frey, good and generous to a fault, is the god of fertility, and carries an erect phallus' (ibid:106).

For the aims of this research it is important to underline that 'it is Thor, rather than Odin who has the place of honour in the temple at Old Uppsala' (Logan 1991:23). This points out to the importance of the farmers and peasants for the Norwegian society. Even this representation reasons the romanticization of the farmer as the national hero in Norway as oppose to the Danish-influenced urban aristocrats.

Besides the warrior and adventurous merchant Vikings, there remained at home the farmers, hunters, fishermen and trappers who provided the resources that made the voyages practicable. The ships had to be built, equipped and provisioned; and the supplies had to be accumulated for the winter months, and so had the commodities required to make up the cargoes of the traders. That's why 'no true picture of the Vikings and their achievements can be gained without some understanding of those providing the economic background in Scandinavia' (Graham-Campbell 2001:10). Even at the time of glorious Viking warriors, peasants still had a significant role for the maintenance of the Scandinavian, and the Norwegian, society. This point will be referred to later in the context of construction of the national hero as the farmer.

The most easily and widely understandable symbol of the Vikings are their ships. They were not uniform; rather there were many kinds of Viking ships varying not only in size (from about 6 metres to about 25 metres) but also in means of power (oars or sail/oars) and in purpose (local, North Atlantic, fishing, commerce, warfare) (Logan 1991:30). The light, graceful, and speedy Viking ships are national symbols widely used in the representation of ancestors of Norway.

Pictures of these ships can be found in all touristic brochures, country catalogues, and souvenirs.

Eriksen's argument that 'the Vikings were selected as the foundational myth upon which the Norwegian national identity was established' has a significance. He argues that 'since Norway was an underpopulated and poor country on the fringes of Europe with no rich cultural and political history, there was a need to find another element to construct the national identity upon. What's more dramatic is that Norway had only one monumental building, the Nidaros Cathedral in Trondheim, which could hardly be used as a national symbol after the Reformation. Thus, the nation-builders invoked the heritage of the Viking Age, asserting that a direct line extended from the fearless Vikings to later-day Norwegians' (Eriksen 1996). The Viking ships, helmets, and axes, which can be found extensively in every tourist guide, country catalogue and souvenir shop, are suitable to be used as the national symbol since they represent the glorious, warrior and heroic past.

2.3. The Territorial Bond or Homeland

Before starting the analysis of the Norwegian homeland, it is important to underline that this analysis is not about where the nation-state's border is, but instead about the representation of the territory with its lakes, mountains, forests, valleys.

To understand the unique position nature has in the Norwegian self-image, it is not enough to look at the geography and climatic conditions. We have to go back to the nation-building period in the 1800s when national poets wrote poems celebrating the mountains and wide-open spaces, and painters portrayed wild and untamed Norwegian scenery. Norway's national identity gradually took the form of a lifestyle characterized by closeness to, respect for and love of nature, particularly the subarctic mountain landscape requiring great courage, strength and endurance from those who have to survive in it (Eriksen 1996).

Norway is usually described as a land of fjords, long rivers and high mountains stretching more than a thousand miles from high north to south. This green-and-gray-granite kingdom is so thick with hills and mountains, so creased by rivers and fjords, and so high above sea level that it defies men to tame it. But this challenging land had been inhabited well before the Vikings, even in the Ice Age. Such descriptions of the Norwegian homeland aim to establish the continuity and timelessness; and the reference to its 'defiant' character aim to equalize the spirit of the homeland to the spirit of its people.

Two indispensable elements of most nationalist representations of Norway since the 19th century are rooted on the land and the sea which exist together and complement each other: 'Man lives by the sea, draws sustenance from the sea, and makes it serve his needs. The sea is not only his highway of commerce, his connective link with the lands which lie beyond; it is also his most dependable source of nourishment. 'Norway has plenty of food –but it is all fish' is exaggeration based on fact' (Scott 1980:5).

Linked to the sea, there is not only fishing but also a 'long', 'honourable', 'proud' and 'rich' tradition in shipping (Fougner 2006:184). So it is no accident that 'Norwegians are leaders in seamanship and have one of the largest merchant fleets of the world' (Scott 1980:5). Norway and Norwegians are depicted as a 'seafaring people' and a 'shipping/ maritime nation' (Fougner 2006:184). In this connection, 'Norwegian shipping' was repeatedly claimed to be a 'significant part of Norwegian culture', and to have 'a cultural-historic status in coastal areas throughout the country' (quoted in Fougner 2006:184).

That a maritime way of life concerned all Norwegians was made clear also in the opening paragraph of the maritime white paper's preface: 'In Norway, people have always lived by the sea, of the sea and on the sea' (St.meld. 1995-96:3). The representation of a seafaring nation can be found in two periods of shared national glory in the past: golden age of sail shipping in the latter half of the 19th century, and the more distant shipping of the Viking age (Fougner 2006:189). In the maritime white paper, the maritime culture was described as the essential bond among the Norwegian people: 'Norwegians are people sharing not any culture, but a maritime culture; not any traditions, but maritime traditions; not any history, but a maritime history; and not any ancestry, but a maritime-related ancestry. The relationship to the sea is a key characteristic of what Norway and Norwegians really are and seemingly always have been' (ibid:186). The opening paragraph of the white paper's preface underlines the vitality of the sea and ocean for the Norwegian national identity: 'Without sea and ocean, Norway and Norwegians would have been something else than what we are' (St.meld. 1995-96:3).

The importance of living by the sea and living on the sea for the Norwegian national identity can also be found extensively in the Norwegian government reports. Svein Ludvigsen, Minister of Fisheries and Coastal Affairs, stated that 'Living by the sea, and 8 out of 10 Norwegians do so, is a national identity' (Ludvigsen 2004:1). This argument is also supported by an interview with a policymaker from the Norwegian Ministry of Fisheries, who defined the most important elements of Norwegian identity as 'being in the periphery of Europe, being a northern country, a country which is sparsely populated, dependent upon trade with other countries, fishing sector and shipping sector have always been important; we have always been seafarers which brought us into contact with other people and other parts of the world' (Tanil, forthcoming book).

To summarise, one can see in the 19th century Norwegian history that the reference to the 'land of ours' was often made after the first declaration of independence in Eidsvoll Constitution. After that the land and all those natural surroundings acquired national meaning and national possession, and started to penetrate national sentiments into people. In other words, certain diacritical markers like mountains, cold climate and the inheritance from the age of the Sagas were nationalised (Neumann 2002:93). The artists and intelligentsia of this nation-building period focused on the homeland and the natural surroundings in order to create them as national identity elements.

In Grieg's work, for instance, landscape often functions as a static, contemplative musical object that plays a central role within the internal structural discourse of his work. For him, 'landscape is not only concerned with pictorial evocation, but is a defining element of his ideology or culture of sound' (Grimley 2006:8). Another example is the poem by Andreas Bull from 1774 which exhorts fellow Norwegians 'not sickly to crawl down to the countries of the South, where your ancestors bashed in so many skulls, but to populate your fatherland as a healthy and respected neighbour; and if you have to go (South), then go, but do not call yourself a Norwegian!' (quoted in Neumann 2002:93).

2.4. The Idea of Norwegian People

Neumann argues that there exist two cultures in Norway: 'one autochthonous people's culture and one foreign civil servant culture' (Neumann 2002:97). At the period of nation-building process, the goal was to eliminate Danish cultural residue by giving superiority to the *folk* and the *folkways*.

Early interest in folkways, i.e. collection of national costumes, old songs, and old myths, in Norway can be found during the first decade of the 19th century. Indeed, Nicolai Wergeland, a minister, interested in folkways, presents the hero in his historical scripts as the populace, the 'people' rather than the Danish-influenced, administrative civil servant stratum. The mark off point for the culturally and ethnically defined Norway was concerned with 'the people's culture', and 'the people' was installed as a key referent of the nation (ibid:96).

An important part of the nation-building process in the 19th century consisted of defining a national culture clearly separate from that of neighbouring countries, which was unique, and which fused the inhabitants into a united people with a common culture and spirit. For nationalistically-minded Norwegians it was especially important to prove that Norway was markedly different from Denmark and Sweden because they were the country's closest neighbours with a language and culture much like Norway's. In fact many believed that Danes, Swedes and Norwegians had so much in common that they made up one Scandinavian nation. This view was naturally disputed by the Norwegian nationalists (Eriksen 1996).

In order to create the idea of the Norwegian people and the culture, nature and veneration of nature were used. National poets wrote poems celebrating the mountains and wide-open spaces, and painters portrayed wild and untamed Norwegian scenery. Norway's national identity gradually took the form of a lifestyle characterized by closeness to, respect for and love of nature, particularly the subarctic mountain landscape requiring great courage, strength and endurance from those who have to survive in it. Danes and Swedes were in this light refined and decadent city people, and the image of the thoroughly healthy, down-to-earth, nature-loving Norwegian was established as a national symbol. Norway's unspoiled countryside thus became a bearing element in the building of the nation, and the national motto that was adopted, 'United and true until Dovre falls', which refers to a massif in central Norway (Eriksen 1996).

'House and cabin, but no castle', reads a well-known national poem. With these words the poet suggests that Norway is a land of *simple, hardworking people* intimately tied to their ecological surroundings (Eriksen 1996). Indeed, reference to the simple life in nature can be found as early as 1781. Gerhard Schøning, a historian, focused on the *simple and dour life* allegedly led by Norwegians as an ideal to cherish: 'It might characterise us, as a Nation, as an Original, and not turn us into a motley copy of other nations, as we have struggled to become for a while'[13] (quoted in Neumann 2002:92). In this simple and dour life, *a profound love of nature and of the physical* is also visible, expressing itself in literature and art, in competitive sports and hiking, bicycling, boating and skiing in the high fields (Scott 1980:10).

However, this simple and dour life has been disturbed by brief intervals of resistance and fight against occupation and foreign domination – whether it is the Danish, Swedish or German. Cherishing independence, Norwegians fought at such times as they did in the Viking past. As Schøning wrote in the 1781, with reference to a battle in 1611 where Norwegian peasants ambushed and massacred a detachment of Scottish mercenaries, the course of the battle 'may serve as Proof, that the Fire and the Heat, the Bravery and the Endurance, which in olden Days made the Norwegians a Terror, almost for all of Europe, is still glowing in the Hearts of Norwegian Peasants[14]' (quoted in Neumann 2002:92). The passion for independence, for a simple and dour life in nature was combined with the fire and heat, bravery and endurance at times of resistance and war. Therefore, the Viking background was combined with the peaceful life in nature while constructing the idea of the Norwegian people and Norwegian way of life.

---

13   See Gerhard Schøning (1781) Norges Riiges Historie
14   ibid.

The events leading to the independence in 1905 were also used in the construction of the image of the Norwegian people: 'Subsequent representations of 1905 invariably stressed the dissolution of the union as an act which followed not a military campaign, not even the policy of the Norwegian state, but which came as the peaceful result of the people's struggle for independence. Hence as a result of the initiative and leading role taken by the nationalists on the issue of independence and the way it was finally achieved, a crucial convocation was established between the terms 'people', 'democracy' and 'independence' (Neumann 2002:102).

As Neumann points out, a crucial link between the terms of people, democracy and independence was established by the Norwegian nation-builders by referring to the events of 1814, 1905, and later 1945; and this link has been deeply knitted in the Norwegian national identity.

2.5. Invented Traditions

National Political Institution: Storting

Norwegian political history has been dominated by different forms of assemblies. The earliest example was the *open-air meetings* held at fixed times and locations in order to arbitrate disputes, condemn lawbreakers, select the king, and do legislation. Later, larger *district assemblies* were developed where all freemen who were entitled to bear arms were entitled to participate (Lindal 1981).

However, in the 12th and especially 13th centuries *aristocratic state assemblies* or *national assemblies,* which were dominated by aristocrats, replaced these old assemblies. These sometimes included representatives of the farmers, but the farmers' influence in them was limited. The 14th century saw the development of *state councils*, which were even more exclusively aristocratic than the national assemblies. These councils superintended the appointment of kings, and administered the state when the throne was vacant. Beyond this, they served as advisory bodies in connection with important decisions made in the name of the crown, especially judicial and legislative decision (ibid).

Later, the formation of the *estate assemblies* provided some balance to the system by bringing together the representatives of the four estates: nobles, clerics, burghers, and farmers. They did not meet regularly, but were convened when the king and the state council wanted special support, particularly in connection with tax increases (ibid).

The political development resulted in the composition of the National Parliament, *Storting,* in the 19th century. From a constitutional point of view, the national struggle against Sweden and the union took the form of a struggle between the Parliament and the King. From 1814 to 1884, the split in the country involved the king, his bureaucracy and his government on the one hand, and the national Parliament on the other. Storting became the natural ally of the nation in the fight to remove the foreign control. Finally Storting emerged as victor in 1884, when the Swedish King was forced to accept the parliamentary principle of selecting ministers who were acceptable to Storting. Thus, Storting gained a heroic image in public's mind due to its resolute and undaunted position against the Union and its King; and this brought about a strong public loyalty to Storting.

Storting have also had an important role in promoting democracy and peace. In 1890 the Norwegian Storting was the first parliament to pass (with a large majority) a resolution in favour of general arbitration treaties, and in the same year, it sent delegates to the first universal Interparliamentary Conference. Owing to this policy, it was entrusted with a highly honourable task in the work for peace. When the Swedish industrialist Alfred Nobel in his will bequeathed his vast fortune to awards for achievements in literature and science, he included a prize for peace work. The awarding of this prize (The Nobel Peace Prize) he left to a committee appointed by the Norwegian Storting, and this committee began its work in 1901. All these bold actions taken by the Storting enabled it to gain a strong foothold and a considerable loyalty, giving way to its heroic representation in the nation's eyes.

It is significant to underline a few points here in order to draw attention to the importance of the Norwegian Parliament for the construction of the Norwegian national identity:

1) First of all, the Norwegian national parliament, Storting, predates the establishment of the Norwegian nation-state. Even before gaining its independence, Norway had a working parliament, which attained strong support and loyalty among the Norwegian public. Therefore, the national parliament, Storting, is considered in this research not as an element representing 'the state', rather as an element representing 'the nation'. In other words, Storting is considered here not as nation-state's political institution, but as a 'national' institution.

2) Secondly, it is equally important to underline that the date celebrated as the national day, May 17th, is not 1905, the year of independence, rather it is 1814, which is the date of signing Eidsvoll Constitution which represents 'the people's rule' rather than 'the King's ruling'. The celebration of that day which is associated to the victorious fight of the national parliament, Storting, signifies not only the institutional but also the emotional and identity-related linkage to it among the Norwegian public. For this reason, Norwegian Parliament, Storting, is considered in this research as an element of the Norwegian national identity, rather than as an institution of the Norwegian state.

3) Finally, the approach employed in this research is the thick constructivist approach rather than the thin one (while the former tries to explode the myths associated with identity formation, the latter threats identities as possible causes of action). Employing a thick constructivist approach, not only the political-institutional functions, but also the identity-politics related and identity-constructive functions of the Norwegian national parliament are considered and analysed here.

As a conclusion, Norwegian political culture has always had democratic and participatory characteristics from its early history up till today, and the Storting acted as the representative and the champion of this political culture. Storting with its link to 'the people', 'democracy' and the principle of 'rule by the people' appears as an important element of the Norwegian national identity. Storting's representation of the people and the people's rule can be found both in the struggle in 1814 against the union and its king, and in the debates on Norway's EU-membership. While in the former the prevailing discourse was the 'rule by the people' against 'the King's ruling', in the latter the discourse was 'the rule by the people' against 'to be ruled by Brussels'. These representations clearly demonstrate the functioning of the national identity dynamic against a perceived threat to its existence.

National Language: A Bilingual Nation

During the Danish rule from 1536 until the signing of the Eidsvoll Constitution in 1814, Norway was governed and administered by an elaborate bureaucratic network recruited from Danish or Danish-educated elite. Danish thus naturally became the language of administration and education, and the Norwegian language's 'nationality' disappeared. Norwegian language persisted, but without its nationality and without its 'Norwegianness'; so the task for the national elite of the 19th century was to rehabilitate the 'nationality' of the Norwegian language.

The advent of cultural nationalism in Norway prompted a desire to dissolve the cultural residue of the previous imperial connection by divorcing the national language from Danish. Danish was the written language in Norway until the middle of the 19th century, there was no printing press in Norway until the 1780s, no university until 1811 (Norwegian officials studied at the University of Copenhagen), and writers moved to Denmark. The provincial capital Christiania, named after the Danish King, was given a Norwegian K only in the 1890s and became Oslo as late as 1928.

In the 1830s and 1840s the force of cultural nationalism threw up 3 literary figures: Henrik Wergerland, Peter Christen Asbjørnsen, and Jørgen Moe. They collected folk stories related to them by ordinary folk in a variety of Norwegian dialects. What they wrote was in practice Danish with 'Norwegianism', the idea being to search for the Volkgeist, the true spirit of the nation. The Norwegian national language (Folkesprog) thus became particularly mythicised and charged with the force of national legitimacy.

'On Our Written Language', written by Ivar Aasen in 1836, was the first systematic expression of what might be called the linguistic patriotism toward the Norwegian language. Aasen explains his motivation for this study as such: 'The point of departure for 'On Our Written Language' is no departure at all. It is a return. After our ancestral land became again what it once was – namely free and independent- it became our obligation to use an independent and national language, given that that is a nation's pre-eminent characteristic' (quoted by Burgess 1999:77). Therefore, a simple, vigorous style recalling that of the Old Norse sagas was tried to be created. Aasen built the new Norwegian literary language on the more conservative and untouched western dialects, and termed this language as *Landsmål,* meaning 'language of the country'. Supported by the efforts of famous Norwegian authors and poets, this literary language gained official recognition in the 1880s.

On the other hand, the 'solemn language' and the middle-class language merged in the south-east, in the course of the century, into a spoken mixed Dano-Norwegian idiom, which was continually Norwegianized. This mixed Dano-Norwegian language was prevalent among the well-educated south-eastern part of the country, mainly around the capital. This language was called *Riksmål*, a term which was initiated by Bjørnson about 1890, and which means 'state-language'. With the systematisation of Riksmål, a Norwegianisation of the educated elite standard, a situation of effective bilingualism was obtained in Norway.

The two languages had contrasting constituencies: Landsmål dominated the countryside, whereas Riksmål prevailed among the educated urban classes. Both, however, sought to develop a Norwegian identity –a national identity- by contrasting means. Landsmål involved a radical bottom up approach of deriving legitimacy from the grass roots; Riksmål worked more gradually from the top down. Later the official names of the two languages became *Nynorsk* meaning 'Neo-Norwegian' for Landsmål, and *Bokmål* meaning 'the book-language' for Riksmål.

For the romantic nationalists of the 19th century the issue was to weld the nation under the banner of a common language. For instance, Halvdan Koht, who later became foreign minister, gave a speech in 1895 by saying that: 'The language issue is going to be the banner under which we are going to unite the Norwegian people. And then, when we really are one people, then we are going to fight for independence, and then we are going to win.' (quoted in Neumann 2002:98) However, there was a clash on which language was to be chosen as the common banner. Populist nationalists advocated the invented language of Ivar Aasen, which to them was the real language of the real people, who has survived despite the state-building efforts of the foreign-born civil servants and their descendants. Statists advocated the language traditionally written and spoken by the civil servant stratum. The clash between them is very well demonstrated in the words of Bjørnson who argued that: 'Norway is split between a 'cultured culture' (dannelseskultur) which was state-bearing, and a 'peasant culture'; between 'inside' and 'outside'; between 'high' and 'low'; between 'quick' and 'slow'; between 'light' and 'dark'; between town and country –particularly between capital-where and else-where. And the decisive and limning criterion for whether one is 'inside' or 'outside' is exactly language –that is the 'language of the realm'' (quoted in Neumann 2002:98).

This split has never been overcome; Norway still remains a bilingual nation. The two languages with their different geographic and cultural features dominated both the nation-building process of the 19th century, and later the 1972 and 1994 debates on EC/EU-membership. In these debates the country was divided between people-bureaucracy, centre-periphery, rural-urban; and these sides took contrasting positions towards the EC/EU membership. Therefore, one can argue that in the context of language 'the other' is not to be found outside the country, rather it is to be found inside, i.e. the other has been the language and the culture of the foreign-educated bureaucracy. The significance of the 'pure', 'Norwegian' national culture and national language against the foreign-influence was to be found both in the nation-building process and in the 1972 and 1994 debates on EC/EU membership.

National Flag

The earliest known flag which could be described as a national flag of Norway is the one used today as the Royal Standard. Eirik Magnusson used a flag described as a golden lion with axe and crown on red, and from 1280 onwards this has been the flag of Norway and of the King of Norway. It was later used on ships and on fortresses until it was gradually phased out during the 17th and 18th centuries.

From about the 16th century until 1814 Norway used the same flag as Denmark, as it was in union with that country. In 1814 after gaining independence from Denmark, Norway adopted the Danish flag with the Norwegian lion in the upper square at the hoist. It was called the 'Dannebrog', which means 'Danish cloth', but whose symbolic meaning can best be described as 'the spirit of Denmark'. This flag was in use until 1821.

In 1844 a union badge combining Norwegian and Swedish colours was placed at the hoist of both countries' flags. The badge was popularly called *Sildesalaten* (the herring salad) from its resemblance to a herring salad. Initially, the union flag was popular in Norway, since it clearly denoted the equal status of the two united states. But as the union with Sweden became increasingly less popular, the Norwegian parliament abolished the union badge from the national (merchant) and state flags in 1899. At the dissolution of the union in 1905, the badge was removed from the navy flag as well.

The first attempt to have a distinctive Norwegian flag was made by Fredrik Meltzer, a member of Storting in 1821. His choice of a Nordic cross was based on the tradition established by the other Nordic countries, Denmark and Sweden; and three colours (red, blue and white) were an inheritage from the free countries of Europe in the 19th century: 'Three colours that now denote freedom, such as we have seen in the French flag of freedom, and still see in that of the Dutch and Americans, and in the Union of the English'. On the other hand, the red and blue colours also explicitly referred to Denmark and Sweden, i.e. former and present union partners. In the final flag, it was agreed to take the red basic colour from Denmark, the blue cross to represent Sweden, and the white frame around the cross to make it the tricolour of freedom, which would place Norway among other free nations. This new Norwegian flag was first flown in 1899.

As a conclusion, the Norwegian flag had times of Danish and Swedish influence, and after the independence it continued carrying both of these influences together with the devotion to freedom on a par with other free and independent nations of Europe. Construction of the Norwegian flag, in this context, has both links to the powerful and dominant neighbours and the union partners, i.e. Denmark and Sweden, and a strong reference to freedom and independence. Therefore, 'free/independent but connected' might be a good expression of the idea behind the construction of the Norwegian flag.

National Anthem 'Yes, we love this country'

The lyrics of the Norwegian national anthem were written by the great patriot, Bjørnstjerne Bjørnson, in 1859, and the melody was written by his cousin Rikard Nordraak in 1864.

The national anthem is in content essentially historical, though there is also some description of the Norwegian landscape. It is also coloured by Bjørnson's great eloquence, his marvellous faculty for rousing the enthusiasm of the masses with a few striking words. He wrote it when he was beginning to embark on that career as a public speaker for which he is renowned in Norwegian history. Typical of Bjørnson is his daring to begin a poem with the little, everyday word 'Ja' ('Yes'). There is also a powerful forward looking pledge to follow the example of those forebears who fought victoriously for Norway in times of distress.

Ja, vi elsker dette landet (Yes, we love this country) starts with the profound love for the Norwegian homeland and its landscape: 'Yes, we love this country as it rises forth, rugged, weathered, above the sea, with the thousands of homes'. In this way, it conveys how much Norwegians love their rugged, coastal nation and all its folk tales. Then the expression 'Farmers their axes sharpened wherever an army advanced, even women stood up and fought as if they were men' demonstrates the devotion to the freedom and independence, and the will of 'the people' to defend their countries. The same adherence to the cherished independence is signified by the expression 'When we were tested sometimes and it was at stake, we would rather burn our land than to declare defeat'. So it evokes and eulogizes the history, traditions and struggles of its people.

Thus Bjørnson has combined in one song devotion and enthusiasm, modesty and strength. Bjørnson put it this way: 'Our National Anthem is that of a small, peace-loving nation, but if it is sung in the hour of danger, determination clad in armour speaks from every line'. Comparing Nordraak's setting of his poem with other National Anthems, Bjørnson said: '...either they make a melancholy impression or else they breathe insurrection, or, alternatively, they are pure idylls. But this National Anthem of ours is free and open as the day, it soars upwards without a threat, it shows determination unmarred by boasting'.

'Ja, vi elsker' became Norway's National Anthem on May 17 1864, the 50th anniversary of the adoption of the Constitution which the people of Norway gave to themselves. It was sung for the first time on that day at Eidsvoll; Bjørnson was a guest at the solemn ceremony along with the Norwegian Government and Parliament. Then it became part of the school text all over the country and was sung by them in children's parades on every 17th of May.

Through the years there have been many occasions when this anthem has acted as a strong, collective voice and as a unifying hymn for the Norwegian people. For instance, it was used during the World War II by the Norwegian resistance which resulted in the German occupants officially forbade any use of the anthem.

To summarize, in the construction of the Norwegian national anthem, all primary characteristics of the national identity, i.e. Norwegian landscape ('rugged, weathered, above to the sea'), Norwegian history (2nd stanza), character of the Norwegian people, that is small, peace-loving nation, but in the hour of danger, determinately clothed in armour ('farmers their axes sharpened wherever an army advance' and 'even women stood up and fought as if they were men'), were touched upon carefully. These descriptions were used as distinctive elements of the Norwegian national identity by one of its most important constructors, Bjørnson. On whether the anthem fulfilled its goal, that is the mobilization of the national identity dynamic, it can be said that the goal is obviously attained since the national anthem has been a unifying hymn at important times and events, for instance, during the resistance to the German occupation.

National Day

There are good grounds for regarding 17th of May, the day of signing the Eidsvoll Constitution, as the pre-eminent date in Norway's history. First of all, it was important for that after centuries as a dependency, Norway once again joined the ranks of free states as an independent realm.

Secondly, it was important for presenting the union with Denmark as an intermezzo in the Norwegian history, with no influence on the inner development of the country. Indeed, the President of the National Assembly, Georg Sverdrup, ended the solemn proceedings with a short and powerful speech where linked the old free Norway to the Norway which was now emerging: 'Thus within Norway's boundaries is resurrected Norway's ancient seat of Kings, which was graced by Athelstans and Sverres and from which, with wisdom and might, they ruled over Norway of old' (quoted in Mykland 1996).

Finally, that date was important for that with the Eidsvoll Constitution Norway emerged with a more liberal Constitution than any other contemporary state. While other free constitutions in Europe, drawn up during the Revolutionary and Napoleonic eras, were rescinded and substituted by more authoritarian regimes, the Norwegian Constitution was made by 'a selection of men from all parts of the realm, of all ranks and dialects, men from court circles as well as landowners who come together in no set order for the sacred purpose of laying the foundations for the rebirth of the nation' (quoted in Mykland 1996).

As early as the 1820s people started to celebrate the 17th of May in grateful memory of the achievements of the Eidsvoll Assembly, the free constitution, and national independence. Since then this day has been established as Norway's National Day or Norway's Liberation Day, which has become a regular festival all over Norway. The efforts of the great poet Henrik Wergeland were also significant in constructing the 17th May as the national day: 'He never tired of praising Norway's free constitution; and wanted to make it a living reality in the people's mind, not only a memory, and also to impress on them their obligation to make further progress and build on the foundations laid at Eidsvoll' (Midgaard 1963:79).

Although Norway gained its full independence on 7 June 1905, national day still remained as the 17th May, the day of the Eidsvoll Constitution for the reasons stated above.

During the German occupation between 1940 and 1945, the 17th of May celebrations were strictly forbidden, but there can scarcely have been any time when the day occupied a more important place in the national consciousness than in the occupation period. Nordahl Grieg explains the longing for independence in a poem: 'Now stands the flagpole bare, Behind Eidsvoll's budding trees, But in such an hour as this, We know what freedom is' (quoted in Mykland 1996).

Therefore, it can be concluded that the construction of the national day as 17th of May is related to the implications of the Eidsvoll Constitution for the Norwegian history and the people: It represents independence after a 400-year union; presents this union as an intermezzo in the Norwegian history and links the old free Norway to the new one; and represents a democratic Constitution made by the participation of 'the people' from all ranks and parts of the country. The designation of the national day based on these implications fulfils the same goals found in the construction of the Norwegian history, language, and culture: Treatment of the union with Denmark as an intermezzo with no significant impact on the real, pure Norwegian elements; strong reference and links to the concept of 'the people' rather than the statesmen; and democracy understood as 'the people's rule' are all seen in the construction of Norwegian national identity elements.

National Hero: Farmer

For the Norwegian nationalists throughout the 19th century the theme of the peasant-farmer as the sustainers of the Norwegian tradition was a central metaphor. During the nation-building process the focus was on the peasants as the real carriers of the nation. It is the farmers who are the nation's 'saviours' – those who have, for one reason or another, preserved the true Norwegian national heritage and who are best qualified to take on the work of building the nation. Thus, in the place of the heroes of old, Norway built a new entourage of heroes: the farmers.

Peasants have always had a special status in the Norwegian society. In the Viking Age Norway, the majority of farmers were independent yeomen, among whom there was a relatively high degree of political and economic equality (Lindal 1981:31). Although with the Middle Ages and the Danish rule, yeoman farmers were forced into tenancy in ever-increasing numbers, they were still largely free due to the lack of a powerful centre. They usually rented their lands on a lifetime basis and enjoyed a free status on their land. Jacob Aall writes in 1809 that: 'Peasant and Freeman make up the lion's share of the Country's Census, and who can deny that they have possessed a Freedom and savoured a Happiness, which is rare in Europe. Who were freer and less taxed than the Norwegian Peasant?' (quoted in Neumann 2002:93).

This image was further strengthened by the writings of the intellectuals of the age, when Schøning wrote with reference to a battle in 1611 where Norwegian peasants ambushed and massacred a detachment of Scottish mercenaries, and described the course of the battle 'as Proof, that the Fire and the Heat, the Bravery and the Endurance, which in olden Days made the Norwegians a Terror, almost for all of Europe, is still glowing in the Hearts of Norwegian Peasants'[15] (quoted in Neumann 2002:92). Some further interpretations also added to this heroic role. For example, Aasen honours the Norwegian farmers as keepers of the language untouched for centuries: 'The farmer has the honour of being the language's saviour; we should therefore listen to his words' (quoted in Burgess 1999:86).

Therefore, the farmers were used as the symbol of the Norwegian national identity due to (1) their relative freedom throughout the Norwegian history, (2) their role in the fight for the liberation of the country, (3) their being the language's saviour, (5) their being the carriers of the pure, untouched Norwegian culture. Such a heroic representation of the Norwegian farmers resulted in their participation in the political life in 1833 with 45 members in the Storting as against 38 officials and 17 merchants. Neumann argues that 'the peasant was a raw material out of which everybody who sought an image for representing 'true Norwegianness' picked certain traits, and forgot about others' (Neumann 2000:250). So, the peasant figure was used to represent the Norwegian people in the construction of the traditions during the nation-building process in the 19th century.

3. The Role of National Art and Literature in the Construction and Institutionalization of the Norwegian National Identity

Norway in the 19th century faced the task of developing a national identity in culture, literature, arts, and theatre. Although Norwegian folk tunes, folk dances, paintings and woodcarvings had being used for many centuries in the rural parts of the country, the realisation of them in the Danish and Swedish influenced urban parts of the country was not until the awakening of the national romanticism of the early 19th century. In the nation-building process patriotic intellectuals exalted and 'nationalised' the Norwegian cultural traditions.

The art and literature also served as the means of internalization/ institutionalization of the national identity among the wide public. Edvard Munch, Edvard Grieg, Bjørnstjerne Bjørnson, and Henrik Ibsen played a crucial role in establishing and institutionalizing Norway's cultural/national identity. They can be seen as pioneers assuming a 'national voice' on behalf of the Norwegian nation.

---

15   See Gerhard Schøning (1781) Norges Riiges Historie

3.1. Art

Edvard Munch (1863-1944) left his mark on the Norwegian cultural politics as a nation builder. His nation-building efforts are most significant in his Aula paintings which he painted on the walls of the Festival Hall of The Royal Frederik's University (today known as the University of Oslo) between 1910 and 1916. As the first major national public art commission after the independence, the Festival Hall paintings carry substantial ideological importance.

A series of paintings surrounding the walls of the Festival Hall were named as *Chemistry, History, New Rays, Women Reaching Toward the Light, Awakening Men in a Flood of Light, The Sun, Spirits in the Flood of Light, Men Reaching Toward the Light, Women Harvesting, Alma Mater, The Fountain*. Munch identified the theme of his painting cycle, Aula, as both 'the great universal forces of eternity' and 'Norwegian' suggesting the convergence of cosmology with the collective historical identity of Norway (Berman 1997:217).

The Sun dominates the front wall of the Festival Hall, and represents the long-cherished independence. In this painting Munch depicts the Norwegian landscape as a fiord with rocky mountains and seaside houses, and the sun rises over this landscape. *Awakening Men* is placed to the left of The Sun painting, and it describes a nation that is awakened from its long slumber. In the painting Norwegian men are depicted as rising to the bright sky with bright hopes for the future.

History and *Alma Mater* are monumental peasant paintings that dominate the side walls of the Festival Hall. These images are 'carefully constructed legacies of the 19th century national rhetoric, and by describing the Norwegian cultural setting they serve as ethical models for future generations of Norwegians' (ibid:213).

History is a 'symbol of acculturation': the oral transmission of knowledge flowing from old man to boy assures cultural continuity and historical consciousness (ibid:217). *Alma Mater* alludes to the 'generalised image of motherhood': she sustains the nation through her fertility. In the painting the young peasant woman sits enthroned in a verdant field, flanked by children, birch trees, and a lake. Her breasts flow with milk, providing the symbolic outlet for the land's sustenance of the people (ibid:217). As the old man in History acculturates, Alma Mater naturalizes her children. The dual features of the Norwegian identity –historical record and nurturing topography- are displaced onto these two bodies. While Alma Mater extends horizontally across the fields, History acts as a mediator between earth and sky, and vertically through time, among generations. The man, paired with the oak, symbolizes the roots, and the woman the soil, for the ongoing national genesis.

These gendered enforcers of national consciousness also reside in landscapes that reinforce their generative functions, for the landscapes are themselves gende-

Picture 1: The Sun (1911) Oil on Canvas 455 x 780 cm
Copyright © The Munch Museum / The Munch-Ellingsen Group / BONO, Oslo 2011

Picture 2: Awakening Men (1911) Oil on Canvas 455 x 305 cm
Copyright © The Munch Museum / The Munch-Ellingsen Group / BONO, Oslo 2011

Picture 3: History (1911) Oil on Canvas 450 x 1163 cm
Copyright © The Munch Museum / The Munch-Ellingsen Group / BONO, Oslo 2011

Picture 4: Alma Mater (1911) Oil on Canvas 455 x 1160 cm
Copyright © The Munch Museum / The Munch-Ellingsen Group / BONO, Oslo 2011

red. As the geographer Donald William Meining notes 'every mature nation has its symbolic landscapes'. The granite cliffs of the Oslo fjord upon which History's old man sits can be described as 'strong', 'powerful', and 'imposing'; while the gentle mountain landscape in which Alma Mater suckles her child can be described as 'fertile and sheltered', 'gently rounded', and 'inviting'. So it can be argued that in these paintings the landscapes that Munch provided for the nation's father and mother were interpreted.

Munch constructed his painting cycle for the university with the greatest thought to the public didactic role that it would assume. He understood the purpose of the public painting, and especially painting at the service of the nation, to be a reintroduction and affirmation of known experience as an invocation the future. Munch also understood that the past was invented and configured by the needs and desires of the present. When he shaped his peasant motifs, he did so with the knowledge that they were among Norway's most potent national symbols, and most heavily mediated images. Frederick Stang, in a lecture delivered in the New Festival Hall on September 6, 1911 said that: 'Here our history, our language, our folk poetry, was retrieved from oblivion... While the farmers conquered the meeting hall, the culture of our farmer-tradition had become a river flowing through our new art and science and scholarship' (quoted in Berman 1997:222). Referencing the Norwegian peasantry, Munch re-enacted the invention and consolidation of a tradition that his intellectual predecessors had practiced in the 19th century.

3.2. Music

The construction of a Norwegian musical style during the 19th century was a function of a broader process of cultural and political self-determination in which folklorism played a central role. Folklorism and music, thus, became powerful nationalist discourses with broad popular appeal (Grimley 2006:25).

Waldemar Thrane's comic opera, Fjeldeventyret (The Mountain Tale) is the earliest expression of the idealization of the Norwegian landscape figures in 1825. It is described by Grimley 'as an important strategy in the definition of an independent self-identity' (ibid:26-31). The sense of Norwegianness in Fjeldeventyret is constructed on a series of binary dualisms: 'the opposition of peasant dialect and the official Danish-Norwegian language; the stylized evocation of Norwegian folk music with nature associations versus a normative contemporary European musical discourse; a rural folk milieu versus an urban audience; retrospective versus prospective visions of Norwegian nationhood; isolationist versus assimilationist nationalist tendencies' (ibid:31).

Therefore, the relationship between music and landscape in Fjeldeventyret can be understood as forming a basic model for Norwegian cultural nationalism through the 19th century. As it has been discussed in the context of the 'idea of the Norwegian people', 'national hero as the farmer', and 'the language issue', these dualities dominate the Norwegian political-cultural domain during the nation-building process of the 19th century; and they are still alive to a certain degree in today's Norway.

In 1848 Ludvig Mathias Lindeman was granted a stipend from an official academic authority, Det akademiske Kollegium, 'to bring to light the despised and unappreciated folk tunes from the branches of the mountains (quoted in Grimley 2006:36). Lindeman's major collection, 'Older and Newer Norwegian Mountain

Melodies', initially containing 540 melodies, was published between 1853 and 1863. Many of the melodies were notated during a series of government-funded trips to Valders, Telemark, Hardanger and Hallingdal. These rural regions were the parts of the country that embodied Norwegian musical and linguistic purity the oldest and hence the most 'authentic' Norwegian folk music could be found (folk music in the central and eastern regions, around Christiania (Oslo) and the Swedish border, was dominated by more recent dance forms and the waltz which were not regarded as 'Norwegian' in the same way as the dance forms in the south-west) (ibid:36-37).

The music of Edvard Grieg (1843-1907) is significant for the nation-building process at the end of the 19th century. He collected the collections of Norwegian folk tunes and dances and incorporated them into his miniature masterpieces. He once said that he 'dipped into the rich treasures of native folk song and sought to create a national art of this unexploited expression of the folk soul of Norway' (Schechter 1997:4).

Grieg's music is rich in evocations of nature and of open space. Mountain echoes, herding calls or distantly heard folk melodies saturate his work, and are among the most characteristics features of his music. Landscape in Grieg's music sets up dualities of authenticity and musical purity that were especially relevant given contemporary debates about Norwegian identity (Grimley 2006:55).

Grieg's most ambitious work is the *Slåtter*. Grieg wrote the pieces based on Hardanger-fiddle tunes which symbolise for many the essence of 'Norwegian' music. This music had functions in the daily living of the people, such as calling the cows in from pasture, singing lullabies to the children, short songs to aid in daily tasks, and songs to chase away the sadness of spending long months in solitary existence. Thus, the op.72 of Grieg is 'a fusion of the unspoiled original folk tune with his own personal idiom in such a way that the native work is given full play while Grieg draws new creative strength from handling it' (Schechter 1997:7).

The Ballade (Opus 24) is considered by many people to be Grieg's masterpiece. Walter Niemann calls this work 'the most perfect musical embodiment of Norway and Norwegian people, of its agonized longing for light and song, and at the same time the most perfect embodiment in music of Grieg' (ibid:8). The theme is based on a folk song from the Valdres area of Norway entitled 'Den Nordlandske Bondestand'.

Opus 66, the collection of 19 folk tunes, consists of quite short pieces, some not more than a few measures in length, but the condensation of harmonic properties tends to overwhelm the listener. Grieg went up into the Jotunheim Mountains of western Norway to get these tunes himself.

Therefore, in the construction of the Norwegian folk music there was a political and cultural shift away from the *embedsmennstad* (civil servant state) and its associated foreign-influenced culture towards the elevation of a folk culture which was 'both progressive and retrospective in outlook' (Grimley 2006:25). With this aim, musicians turned to the rural areas that remained pure, authentic, untouched, and maintained elements of a pure 'Norwegian' identity. Thrane, Lindeman, Grieg, and many others resorted to Telemark, Hardanger and Hallingdal regions to surface folk tunes from the mountains and to use them as the defining features of the Norwegian national identity.

3.3. Literature

Bjørnstjerne Bjørnson (1832-1910) was a prolific writer of poems, plays, short stories, and novels as well as a dynamic politician and public speaker. He was the first to introduce contemporary peasants into Norwegian literature and his early literary successes came from tales of peasant lives. These spirited peasant romances were thought to give special insight into the Norwegian character. In 1903 he became the first Scandinavian to receive the Nobel Prize for literature (Woertendyke 1997:47).

However, in the field of literature the name which became most widely known was probably the playwright Henrik Ibsen (1828-1906) who chose a Norwegian setting for his dramas. Many of Ibsen plays had a specifically Norwegian theme, and nearly all had a Norwegian domestic setting. In Ibsen plays readers find themselves in a small Norwegian coastal town where social forces and conflicts arising from differing viewpoints (Hemmer 1996).

When creating new Norwegian drama his principal goal was clearly national. Together with his friend and colleague Bjørnson, he founded 'The Norwegian Company' in 1859, an organ for Norwegian art and culture. They had a joint programme for their nationalistic activities. Ibsen was especially concerned with the role of theatre in the young Norwegian nation's search for its own identity. In these 'nation-building' pursuits, he gathered his material from the country's medieval history and perfected his art as a dramatist (ibid). This is prominent in *The Pretenders* which is a story taking place in Norway in the 1200s, a period marked by destructive strife. But Ibsen's perspective is Norway in the 1860s. He expressed his thoughts on national unity as such: 'Norway was a kingdom, now it will be a nation; all shall be as one hereafter, and all shall know in themselves that they are one' (quoted in Hemmer 1996).

Brand and *Peer Gynt* are two rather different twin works of Ibsen, where the focus is on the problem of personality with an underlying message or warning for the nation. In these works Ibsen dramatizes the conflict between a dedication to a demanding lifelong quest, and an opportunistic acting out of an unnatural role.

Brand (1866) takes as its hero an unbending, uncompromising, sternly dedicated to the principle of 'all or nothing'; whereas Peer Gynt (1867) follows the fantastic career of a person wholly unprincipled, buoyant, yielding, and content to adopt as his motto: 'To thine own self be –enough'. While the one is admirable but unlovable, the other is lovable but reprehensible; and yet both can justifiably be considered in part as portraits of the author as well as the nation (Hemmer 1996).

Brand's message is that the individual must follow the path of individual will in order to achieve true humanity and the real freedom. This message can also be read as a message to the nation: it shall rise up culturally and politically. On the other hand, Peer Gynt's message warns his nation of the danger of losing its identity: The ageing Peer looks back upon his wasted life while he peels an onion. He lets each layer represent a different role he has played. But he finds no core. He has to face the fact that he has become 'no one', that he has no 'self'. This message can be read as the reflection of Ibsen's concerns about his nation's self identity.

Towards the end of his life Ibsen admitted to his friend that: 'He who wishes to understand me, must know Norway. The magnificent, but severe, natural environment surrounding people up there in the north, the lonely, secluded life – the farms miles apart- forces them to be unconcerned with others, to keep to their own. That is why they become introspective and serious, they brood and doubt – and they often lose faith. At home every other person is a philosopher! There, the long, dark winters come with their thick fogs enveloping the houses – oh, how they long for the sun!' (quoted in Hemmer 1996).

4. Conclusive Remarks

This chapter aimed to provide a thorough analysis of the 'construction' of the Norwegian national identity in the 19th century. In this context, 5 fundamental composing elements of the national identity were analysed and discussed: history, foundational myth, territory/homeland, idea of people, invented traditions (national political institution, national language, national flag, national anthem, national day, national hero).

It is important to underline once more that the aim of this research is the analysis of the Norwegian 'nation-building' process carried out by the intelligentsia, artists, and politicians in the 19th century rather than the Norwegian 'nation-state building' or simply state-building. For this reason, analysis is mostly carried out in the framework of national identity elements.

To summarize, the construction of the Norwegian national identity took place as follows:

(1) History: The construction of the Norwegian history consists of three parts: a glorious medieval past; decay, loss of independence, and long union with Denmark; and independence in the 19th century. In the period of Norwegian nation-building process, the history of the country was the subject of careful research; and eminent historians wrote scholarly works on medieval Norway, reedited and commented on the Old Norse literature. Their task was to establish continuity in Norwegian history, whereby the state of the 19th century would appear as the legitimate heir to the medieval kingdom. The solution was to resort to the democracy and independence lay hidden in the freedom of the peasant class of the Middle Ages who were the carriers of the historical continuity (Simensen 2000:92). In this way, 'the conception of history presented a continuity of understanding, a principle of national will, and of the realisation of 'national destiny' (Burgess 1999:86).

(2) Foundational myth: The Vikings, described as courageous, strong, violent and passionate at the time of war, were adopted easily as the foundational myth with their virtues and glorious victories. The Viking characteristics were believed to have enabled Norwegian people to live in peace in the wild nature, and to survive by working very hard in the difficult geographic and climate conditions. So at the time of constructing a national identity, the proud, adventurous, glorious, heroic, generous Vikings were a precious foundational myth to resort.

(3) Territory/Homeland: The construction of the national territory is not about where the nation-state's border is, but instead about the representation of the territory with its lakes, mountains, forests, valleys. In the period of nation-building process, reference to the 'land of ours' was often made, and the land and all those natural surroundings acquired national meaning and national possession, and started to penetrate national sentiments into people. In other words, certain diacritical markers like mountains, cold climate and the inheritance from the age of the Sagas were nationalised (Neumann 2002:93).

(4) Idea of people: Nationalist pioneers draw attention to the folkways, and presented the hero as the 'people' rather than the Danish-influenced, administrative civil servant stratum. The mark off point for the culturally and ethnically defined Norway was concerned with 'the people's culture'; and 'the people' was installed as a key referent of the nation. In this regard, the idea of the Norwegian people and Norwegian way of life was constructed referring to the passion for independence, for a simple and dour life in nature, and fire and heat, bravery and endurance at times of resistance and war.

(5) National institution: Norwegian national parliament, Storting, is considered here not as 'nation-state's' political institution, but as a 'national' institution, and signifying not only the institutional but also the emotional and identity-

related elements among the Norwegian public. Norwegian political culture has always had democratic and participatory characteristics from its early history up till today, and the Storting acted as the representative and the champion of this political culture. Therefore, Storting with its links to 'the people', to 'democracy', and to the principle of 'rule by the people' appears as an important element of the Norwegian national identity.

(6) *National language:* Starting from the 19th century, Norwegian language and culture were being nationalized with a desire to dissolve the cultural residue of the previous imperial connection by divorcing the national language from Danish. Aasen built a new Norwegian literary language on the more conservative and untouched western dialects, and termed this language as *Landsmål,* meaning 'language of the country'. On the other hand, a mixed Dano-Norwegian language was prevalent among the well-educated southeastern part of the country, mainly around the capital. This language was called *Riksmål* which means 'state-language'. Landsmål dominated the countryside, whereas Riksmål prevailed among the educated urban classes. Both, however, sought to develop a Norwegian identity –a national identity- by contrasting means. Landsmål involved a radical bottom up approach of deriving legitimacy from the grass roots; Riksmål worked more gradually from the top down.

(7) *National flag:* Norwegian flag had times of Danish and Swedish influence, and after the independence it continued carrying both of these influence together with the devotion to freedom on a par with other free and independent nations of Europe. So the Norwegian flag was constructed with a reference both to the previous union partners and neighbours, Denmark and Sweden, and to the freedom and independence. Therefore, 'free/independent but connected' might be a good expression of the idea behind the construction of the Norwegian flag.

(8) *National anthem:* Norway's national anthem conveys how much Norwegians love their rugged, coastal nation, its proud history and all its folk tales. It evokes and eulogizes the history, traditions and struggles of its people. It has been a unifying hymn at important events, whether happy or sad.

(9) *National day:* 17th of May was established as Norway's National Day in grateful memory of the achievements of the Eidsvoll assembly, the free constitution, and national independence. The date is significant for three respects: after centuries as a dependency Norway once again joined the ranks of free states as an independent realm; the new Constitution presented the union with Denmark as an intermezzo in the Norwegian history; and a selection of men from all parts of the country, of all ranks and dialects prepared this democratic and liberal Constitution.

(10) National hero: Farmers are often regarded as the core of national identity, but Norway is an extreme case of strong idealization of the farmers and fishermen as a symbol of the nation. One reason is that in the 19th century when Norwegian nationalism arose, other socio-economic groups on which national identity could be projected were simply missing: the civil servants were Danish-influenced, the King was Swedish, the urban class was weak, and there was no significant class of noblemen or warriors. So the inventors of the nation (mainly intellectuals) took what they could use: the Vikings (to produce an image of a glorious history of courageous warriors and tradesmen), and the farmers and fishermen in the peripheries of the country as the core of Norwegianness (Hille 2002). But the idea that farmers are the representative of the people does not mean that they are 'the people' –it means exactly that they 'represent' it. Neumann argues that 'the peasant was a raw material out of which everybody who sought an image for representing 'true Norwegianness' picked certain traits, and forgot about others' (Neumann 2000:250).

(11) Art and literature: The folk tunes, folk dances, paintings and woodcarvings that had been used for many centuries in the rural parts of the country, were exalted, and 'nationalised' by means of the efforts of the patriotic intellectuals. In that process, Edvard Munch, Edvard Grieg, Bjørnstjerne Bjørnson, and Henrik Ibsen played a crucial role in establishing and institutionalizing Norway's cultural/national identity.

It is important to underline that what is referred here as 'Norwegianness' is not an objective, qualifiable picture of what it means to be Norwegian, but rather, it is what Hobsbawn and Anderson have identified as 'invented traditions' and 'imagined communities' respectively (Hobsbawn 1983, Anderson 1991). As mentioned before, Hobsbawm's 'invented traditions' means 'a set of practices, normally governed by overtly or tacitly accepted rules and of a ritual or symbolic nature, which seek to inculcate certain values and norms of behaviour by repetition, which automatically implies continuity with the past' (Hobsbawn and Ranger 1983:1), and Anderson's 'imagined political community' is imagined because 'the members of even the smallest nation will never know most of their fellow-members, meet them, or even hear of them, yet in the minds of each lives the image of their communion' (Anderson 1991:6-7).

It is argued in this research that the national identity, and ideas about Self and Other can be so significant for wide public that these abstract notions can influence important foreign policy choices. Next chapter analyses the functioning of the national identity dynamic in relation to a significant foreign policy choice, i.e. Norwegian EC/EU-membership, by referring to these five key elements of the Norwegian national identity.

Chapter 4: Functioning of the Norwegian National Identity Dynamic

1. Introduction

Primarily, this research argues that an analysis of foreign policy choices does not imply an analysis of material facts only, but also the human interpretation (social construction) of these material conditions in any national context. For this reason, it takes an identity politics route by bringing together middle-ground social constructivist approach[16], which explains the impact of the identities and interests on the foreign policy choices, and the individual psychology approach, the 'national identity dynamic'[17], which seeks to answer questions as 'Why large groups of people act together in certain political situations?', 'How do masses mobilize for or against certain foreign policy decisions?', 'Is there a method for explicating the relationship between the mass attitudes and actual foreign policy decisions?'.

To remind it again, it is argued in this research that national identity describes (1) the condition in which a mass of people have made the same identification with national symbols –have internalized the symbols of the nation-, and (2) the possible mass mobilization of this people to act as one psychological group when there is a threat to, or the possibility of enhancement of, these symbols of national identity (Bloom 1990). Chapter 3 analyzed the first part of this theoretical assumption by assessing the construction of the Norwegian national identity in the 19th century through 'construction' and 'internalization' of the symbols of 'the nation'. On this background, Chapter 4 analyzes the second part of this theoretical assumption, namely the 'national identity dynamic', which impacts on foreign policy choices as follows:

1. The mass national public will mobilize if it perceives that there is a threat to, or the opportunity of enhancing, national identity.
2. The mobilization of the mass national public is, by definition, the largest possible mobilization within a nation-state.
3. It is a feature of domestic politics that there is competition to appropriate the national identity dynamic.
4. The national identity dynamic, if mobilized, necessarily influences government decisions (Bloom 1990:132).

---

16   See Marcussen et al. 1999, 2001; Marcussen 2005.
17   See Bloom 1993.

This chapter is devoted to the presentation and discussion of the functioning of the Norwegian national identity when encountered with a perceived threat. Throughout this chapter, views and perceptions of Norwegian people about themselves and Europe, and how compatible or conflictive are these perceptions are presented and discussed thoroughly. The chapter also includes an analysis of the membership negotiations, the political debate over the membership, and the referendum campaigns considering the actors, arguments and results of both 1972 and 1994 referendums.

The goal of the detailed analysis of the arguments of EU-proponents and EU-opponents in this chapter is not to determine which of these arguments are right or wrong. Instead, the actual aim of this analysis is to present (1) the close link between these arguments and the Norwegian identity elements, (2) how Norwegian identity elements were employed in the EU-discourses, (3) how these discourses influenced Norwegian people's perception of themselves and the EU, (4) how these perceptions led to the perception of a threat to the national identity elements, so led to the national identity dynamic to function, and finally (5) how the national identity dynamic in the Norwegian context influenced a major foreign policy choice (EU-membership).

This analysis will also help to overcome the criticism of social constructivist approaches for that 'they fail to provide concrete and testable causal mechanisms through which the process of choosing policies and defining interests takes place' (Moravcsik 1999:671). Therefore, the clear demonstration of the sequence of the causal relationships from (2) to (5) will fill the gap between the identity definitions and the foreign policy decisions, and empirically validate the social constructivist hypotheses.

2. 1961-62: The First Application to the EEC and the First Debate

In a rapidly changing international environment, Britain announced its intention of applying for full membership of the EEC, and submitted its formal application on 9 August 1961. Denmark and Ireland submitted their membership applications immediately after this. The successive applications of close partners opened up the first debate in Norway on the integration with Europe.

For many leading figures within the Labour Government it was clear that Norway could not stay aloof from an organised economic cooperation which included not only the EEC countries, but also the UK and other EFTA countries. However, there was a great resistance towards closer affiliation with the EEC in the Labour

Party, in the Storting, and among the public. After a year of investigations and discussions, on 28 April 1962, the Storting decided to negotiate for membership of the EEC. The reasons of this decision were: the significance of Britain, the fear of becoming locked out of European markets, and the question of access to capital. However, the application started a big debate on the issue, and led to a certain grassroots mobilisation against membership.

The first major institutionalisation of this nationalist movement came in December 1961, when a group of 143 artists and intellectuals, the majority of whom sympathised with the left wing of the Labour Party, formed a 'Movement Against Membership in the Common Market – the 143' even before Storting's decision to negotiate for membership (Neumann 2002:109). The name of the movement represented the civilian resistance to the Nazi occupation during the Second World War. It also latched on to a Norwegian patriotic tradition by addressing itself to 'Norwegian women and men', by declaring itself to be 'the defender of the Constitution' and to protest 'the abandonment of Norway's independence and sovereignty' (ibid:109).

The argument of the opponents was that membership of the EEC would mean a break with Norwegian history and a bypassing of the people:

> 'When the large decisions in the history of our country were taken in 1814, in 1905 and in 1940, a united people stood behind them... The ties that bind us to European culture are strong. However, Europe is two things. There is a Europe which has inspired our work of freedom, our democracy and our Constitution. Yet there is also a Europe which has been responsible for wars of conquest, colonialism as well as economic and social oppression. The danger is great that it will be the latter of these tendencies that is going to envelop us if we join the Common market... As an independent state our country must strengthen the work done in the large world-wide institutions in order to bring all peoples closer to one another, in mutual understanding and cooperation. The new West European union which the Common Market is going to become, does not have such a goal... Our property right and right to govern our own country will be undermined... The acting Parliament does not have the people's mandate to relinquish Norway's sovereignty and national independence for a purpose such as this one... The will of the people must be brought to the fore' (quoted in Neumann 2002:109).

The central concept here was the people and people's rule. Traditionally, Storting had been perceived as the direct representative of the people, i.e. as representing the 'nation' rather than the 'state'. It had also been the case that people's rule spoke through Storting in 1814, in 1905, and in 1940, which gave way to liberation of the 'state' by the 'people'. However, in the 1960s Storting was perceived as a congregation of politicians rather than as a direct representative of the people; so it was argued that the question of Norway's relationship with the EEC should not be decided by the politicians, rather by the people in a referendum. That move signifies the continuity of the historical line of 1814, 1905, and 1940 in that it reflects the clash between 'foreign-influenced civil servant stratum' and 'the Norwegian people', and the people and people's rule being the determining factors for the nation's foreign policy choices. But this time 'the part of the state which is seen as being closest to the people, Storting, was bracketed as standing too far from the people' (ibid:110).

Another important point here was the representation of Europe as being fundamentally dichotomous. With an argument that 'there was a benign cultural Europe of peoples, and a malign Europe of imperialist states; and the Common Market was an institutionalisation of the latter, and it was on its way to becoming a 'union'' othering of the EC was complete against the historical presentation of the Norwegian people's struggle for independence (ibid:110).

The second articulation of the nationalist position came from the Centre Party MP Erik Braadland in the early 1960s:

'Some would even insist that by giving away rights in our own country we may win the same rights in other Common Market countries... (But do we?) Which country has even remotely the same opportunities to hunt and fish as we do? There is no balance between what we give and what we gain... the Norwegian people have built up the modern and affluent society in which we live today. By consistent work and innovation, by going in unison, in national community, we have reached where we are today. It is the feeling of community, popular sovereignty, our national self-government which maintains it, and which is the only thing which can maintain the society we have created... we want to maintain the right to preside over what nature has bestowed on us, and what we have accumulated as production capital, not because we are ungenerous or jingoistic, but because we want to remain a nation' (quoted in Neumann 2002:110).

There was also a reference to the nature with its links to the nation, the people, and society. It was argued that the opportunity to hunt, fish, and harvest had produced the riches of modern Norway. This soil-people nexus was presented under attack and must be defended in order to 'remain a nation'. Therefore, 'we', that is the people, should say no to the EEC (ibid:110).

These arguments and the line of reasoning are significant for the aims of this research at least in three respects:

1. First of all, it demonstrates the functioning of the national identity dynamic for the first time in the post-war period, i.e. after the resistance to the German occupation in the 1940s. Comparing the significance of 'the threat' in both cases, it can be concluded that negative connotation of the 'union' was as strong as the German occupation, so both could trigger the national identity dynamic –although at different degrees.
2. Secondly, it signifies the perception of Europe as the other of the national identity elements. While freedom, democracy, people's rule, and affluent society represent the 'self', colonialism, economic and social oppression, imperialism and free market represent the 'other'. Such a clashing perception could easily trigger the perception of a threat, and it would appear again in the subsequent debates on the EC/EU in Norway.

3. Finally, it can be recognized that all these elements employed in the definition or perception of the self and the other in this debate are those elements composing the Norwegian national identity, i.e. the link between nature, people, society; hunting, fishing, farming; people's rule, democracy, fight for self-control and independence. Presenting arguments based on the national identity elements, and pointing out the threat to these elements, politicians and political activists triggered the national identity dynamic to arise against this perceived threat[18]. This is also confirmed by Sæter who concludes 'the country's economic and social development had produced deeply rooted cultural and moral norms, which many people felt to be threatened by the prospect of a remote and supranational Brussels' (Sæter 1996:134).

When the French president de Gaulle vetoed British membership of the EEC in January 1963, the EEC question disappeared from the Norwegian political agenda as quickly as it had arisen.

3. 1967: The Second Attempt to Get Norway into the EC

The membership issue was not totally out of agenda for Britain. It renewed its application in 1967, and Denmark followed suit within 24 hours. The coalition government in Norway composed of Conservative Party and three centre parties, Liberal Party, Centre Party and the Christian Democratic Party, applied for membership two months later.

The situation in 1967 differed from 1961-62. Domestic political circumstances in Norway had changed, as had the merged European Communities: On the one hand, the intergovernmentalist approach of de Gaulle and the application by Britain eased the Norwegian politicians, indicating that the EC might develop less along Community-based lines than before. On the other hand, Norway in 1967 was governed by a non-socialist coalition which was divided over the issue of EC membership. Upon the membership issue, they did not want to break up the coalition (Archer and Sogner 1998:29). So, the text of the government recommendation of Norwegian membership spoke of a Norwegian application 'as the best means of clarifying the basis for Norway's relations with the EC', not a commitment to joining the EC (quoted in Archer and Sogner 1998:29). Furthermore, like its Labour predecessor, the government made entry conditional on British membership and on satisfactory safeguards for the primary sectors. However, the application was stopped by a French veto against British membership for the sec-

---

18 It is important to underline that what is considered here as 'threat' is not an actual one, rather a perceived threat.

ond time before negotiations had not even reached the preliminary stage. There was no time for a real debate on EEC membership this time.

4. 1972 Debate on EC Membership

4.1. Application Discussions

On 24 and 25 June 1970, the Storting discussed the renewed application to the EC, and approved it 132-17. Norwegian Foreign Minister Stray declared in the formal opening session of the negotiations on 30 June 1970 that 'the Norwegian Government takes a positive position towards a constructive European cooperation which has as its goal the strengthening of Europeans both economically and politically, so that they can play an increasing role in the struggle to strengthen international peace and security' (Miljan 1977:212). However, he also underlined 'the protection of special Norwegian interests in a satisfactory manner'. Bilateral negotiations between Norway and the EC began with the first meeting on 22 September 1970.

4.2. Membership Negotiations

In applying, Norway had to formally accept all decisions taken on the basis of EC's treaties (the acquis communautaire). However, Norway had reservations about adapting to the EC's agricultural and fisheries policies.

Agricultural policy was a central issue when the Norwegian negotiations opened in June 1971. The two sides were far apart. Norway sought to maintain a national agricultural policy within the EC, without adapting to the common agricultural policy (CAP). The agricultural organisations opposed any change in the existing policy pattern and level of production, i.e. no weakening of import controls, no regional arrangements confined to disadvantaged areas, no change in the powers of the producer organisations, and no change in the system of price subsidies. The EC showed some willingness to meet Norway's demands, but it would not concede permanent exceptions from the common agricultural policy. By December 1971 a compromise was agreed which accommodated some of the Norwegian demands; but the exceptions granted were not permanent, and Norway had to adapt to the common agricultural policy.

Fisheries policy was another problematic area. On the day membership negotiations opened in June 1970, the EC concluded a new fisheries agreement providing for non-discriminatory access to member states' fishing limits. This was totally unacceptable to Norwegian fishermen who demanded permanent retention of an exclusive twelve-mile fishing limit around the coast. They also wanted extensive rights of the Norwegian producers' organisations to continue, including compulsory membership, sales rights to the entire catch, and price and regulating rights. Though the EC was willing to make concession to Norway's special needs and interests, and to treat Norway as the special case it claimed to be, it was not prepared to give a legal guarantee that an exclusive twelve-mile zone would continue after the transition period. Neither did it recognise Norway's interests as vital. On 15 January 1972, the EC-Norwegian fisheries protocol was signed; but at home anti-marketeers considered it a capitulation, and the fishermen's national organisation unanimously rejected it. Two days later, fisheries minister Knut Hoem resigned because of the lack of an EC guarantee for the period after 1982.

Accession treaties of Britain, Denmark, Ireland and Norway were all signed in Brussels on 22 January 1972. This provoked an intense debate on the EC-membership in Norway splitting political parties, organizations, institutions, groups and even families into opposing camps.

4.3. Referendum Campaigns

The 1972 EC membership debate in Norway divided both the political arena and the society into two opposing groups. This research focuses on the political and societal actors, i.e. 'ideological entrepreneurs', who led the yes and no campaigns, and on the discourses and the campaign material they used. The aim is to analyse how Norwegian national identity was employed in this debate and how references to Norwegian national identity and the perceived threat gave way to the functioning of the national identity dynamic. To achieve this end, first of all, political and societal actors of the referendum campaign in Norway are presented and clarified; secondly, their arguments and discourses are presented and discussed; and finally the result they created in the public arena, i.e. functioning of the national identity dynamic, are analysed in this section.

Actors

In the Storting vote in June 1970 on the renewal of the 1967 application to the EC, the coalition government was divided into two groups: The Conservatives and some members of the Christian Democrats and the Liberal Party wanted to hold the coalition together and to get Norway into the EC, while seven representatives from the Centre Party and three from the Christian Democrats voted against. The rest of the Centre Party did not want to join the EC, but hoped to achieve this end without destroying the coalition.

The government, divided on the question of EC-membership, resigned on 2 March 1971. The new Labour minority government had its controversies over the question, but it was more united than the coalition government, and was committed to finalise the negotiations.

Meanwhile in the society the anti-EC and pro-EC groups formed their organisations and started their campaigns. The opposition had an advantage over the proponents of membership in that they had started their campaign once Norway's application had been announced, while the pro-EU groups had to await the outcome of the negotiations, adopting a 'wait and see' attitude.

As soon as the Norwegian EC application was reactivated in June 1970 the opposition re-emerged; the 'People's Movement against Norwegian Membership of the Common Market' was established in August 1970. The People's Movement included veterans from the battles fought in 1962 and 1967, as well as observers from each of the political parties' youth organisations. These had all, except for the Young Conservatives, declared themselves opposed to EC membership. The Movement's task was to work against Norwegian membership to the EC, and to supply information to the population. It was largely financed by the agricultural and fisheries organisations, and supported by the students, professors, peasants and urban leftists.

The conclusion of the negotiations in January 1972 boosted the EC proponents, who could finally start their campaign. The Labour Party abandoned its wait and see policy, and the 'Yes to the EC' campaign was initiated in March 1972. They were supported by the big business and the industry, such as the Norwegian Union of Industrialists and the Banking Union, as well as the civil servants, bureaucrats and pro-EC party functionaries.

Arguments

Ingebritsen and Larson (1997:215) argue that in the EC debate Norwegians were deeply divided about their relationship to Europe and 'Europeanness'. Neumann supports this point by arguing that 'the parliamentary debate reflects strong disagreement not so much about what Norway is, but about what Europe and the EC are' (Neumann 2002:112). A clear analysis of the arguments of the both sides of the debate is significant in this regard to clarify the representation of the 'self' and 'other' as fundamentally different identity constructs, which then initiate the national identity dynamic.

First of all, *fundamental values* of Norway and Europe were represented differently by the yes- and the no-side. On the yes-side, it was argued that Europe and Norway are of the same order: 'Norway is just another cultural nation in a European order of cultural nations. It may be a bit more advanced when it comes to democratic rights, including women's rights, it may have a somewhat better social policy, but it is basically a variant on a European theme' (ibid:112). On the no side, it was argued that Norway is basically different from Europe: 'Europe is hierarchical, Norway is egalitarian. Europe is centralised, Norway is dispersed. Europe cares about the strong, Norway cares about the weak' (ibid:112). The history was also used against Europe: 'Norwegian nation-building was successfully portrayed as a question of organising an egalitarian peasant-based stock against a European culture and its local representatives' (ibid:112). In these representations, while yes-side stressed the common denominators between the two, i.e. democracy, social rights, equality, the no-side stressed the clash of values and cultures.

History, i.e. difference in colonial past, was used as another breaking point between the two: First, the no-side made a pairing of cultural and security concerns in a critique of 'neo-colonialism': Norway is different from EC countries in this regard, because 'our country does not find itself in a conflicting relationship with developing countries through colonial or post-colonial investments' (from the Report to Parliament, quoted in Neumann 2002:114). The pros did little to counter this argument except to gesture vaguely in the direction of Norway being seemingly inevitably part of a European culture which despite its colonial past was positive, not negative (ibid:114).

Furthermore, *religion* constituted another break from Europe. Matlary (1993:51) argues that 'the attitude that Norway can be culturally separated from Europe was common in religious circles': 'Traditional anti-Catholicism has faded in urban, educated milieu, but this was not where the Christians were found. In the West and South, fundamentalism, sectarianism, and a pronounced anti-Catholicism were strong. In this context, even the Treaty of Rome was presented as having some connection with the Pope' (Matlary 1993:51).

The most important feature of this mentality is not the primitive anti-Catholicism of the fundamentalist Protestantism, but that the Norwegian brand of Protestantism as a whole allows for a sharp separation of Christianity from its historical European roots. Based on these grounds Christian People's Party opposed the EC membership with such arguments that 'a number of people were worried about the EC closing down the Protestant Norwegian state church', and also feared a 'Catholic invasion' (quoted in Neumann 2002:114).

Economic arguments about the membership (related to agriculture, fisheries, and national resources) were linked to the sovereignty argument which then turned into a question of identity politics. On the one hand, the need to maintain Norwegian resources for the Norwegians was the major glue of the anti-membership alliance; and the slogan was 'No to the sale of Norway' (quoted in Neumann 2002:114). On the other hand, importance of the regional policy, agriculture and fisheries was more related to culture and identity than money. First of all, agriculture and fisheries have been an integral part of Norwegian regional policy which aims to keep a substantial proportion of the population in the periphery. Norwegian agricultural support has been used to promote settlement in areas where there are typically few other employment options. Secondly, farming is closely identified with the early period of nation-building, when the image of the Norwegian farmer was associated with the struggle for the independence of the country. Third, regional policy was linked to the national identity in that: 'There was a nexus between 'Norway' understood as the Norwegian people, and 'Norway' understood as Norwegian territory. If the people do not cover all of the territory, Norway cannot be Norway. Since EC membership will entail centralisation, it will inevitably lead to a drop in rural population, and then the entire idea of Norway will be in danger' (ibid:115).

The EU-proponents objected to such arguments, and defended the growth argument for the Norwegian industry which was well developed and in productivity terms was more important than the agriculture and fishing sectors. However, the EU-opponents subsumed the whole question of economy into what is represented by them as the more basic issue, namely sovereignty and identity politics in favour of a certain idea of Norway. In that context, the yes-side was represented as 'traitors to the nation and the national history'; and marked off as 'the internal enemy'. This representation dates back to the Norwegian nation-building process when the civil servant stratum was branded as the enemy of the Norwegian nation: they were as Arne Garbourg put it in 1883, 'failing their duty to the Norwegian nation, and so they became enemies: the enemy is within the country' (quoted in Neumann 2002:99).

The *representation of 'union'* was also a divisive point between the yes- and the no-side. Prime Minister Bratelli and the pros generally almost without fail referred to the EC as *Fellesskapet* – like its German translation Gemeinschaft, which invokes solidarity, togetherness, and community. They stressed Norway's role as a cultured nation, with a responsibility for the further evolution of that central feature of European civilisation. Their representation of the EC was close to the principle of subsidiarity and the pooling of sovereignty to accomplish the ultimate goals. Prime Minister Bratelli stated in this context that:

> '*The EC should primarily take care of tasks which cannot be handled by one state alone, which cannot be handled by the sovereignty of one state alone. We are talking about a sovereignty which states working together are trying to grapple from yet untamed forces, particularly in international economics. There are forces in our closely integrated world which can only be handled by regional or international sovereignty*' (quoted in Neumann 2002:112).

However, the antis' representation of the union was totally different. By successfully representing the EC as being on its way to becoming a federation, a United States of Europe, membership was presented not only as a question of being dissolved in a larger unit, but also as a question eradicating Norwegian democracy and identity by returning to a situation which existed before, namely a union with stronger parties (ibid:115). They argued that:

> *'Both in 1814 and in 1905, there were unionist parties which held that Norway would benefit from joining larger units. It was the right and the civil servants then. Now it is the Norwegian Union of Industrialists, the Banking Union, civil servants and the party functionaries. On the other hand, there were peasants and leftists, and now a plethora of peripheral groups without established positions of power, and the People's Movement (who support the independence)'* (quoted in Neumann 2002:113).

Therefore, opposing EC-membership was portrayed as an extension of the fight for independence (Bjørklund 1997:149). Referring to the division between 'the nation/ the people' and 'the state/ the government', the People's Movement represented 'the people' rather than the state apparatus as the custodian of sovereignty.

The catchiest move of the no-side was its putting forward terse and easy to understand messages with a clear reference to the Norwegian history and nationalist sentiments. The basic arguments against membership concerned the economic consequences as well as Norwegian sovereignty. In their counter-report to the government's White Paper on Norwegian membership, 'Om Norges tilslutning til De Europeiske Fellesskap', they criticised the Treaty of Rome for its free-market attitudes, and warned that Norwegian membership would take away politicians' control over the economy which would lead to social injustice (Archer and Sogner 1998:33). It was also effective in presenting the dangers or threats of the EC-membership to the Norwegian national identity elements: 'All Norwegian fish would be taken by foreign trawlers; agriculture would be finished; small industries would be ruined and bought up by foreign capital; the north would be depopulated; the country would be invaded by foreign workers, catholic ideas, rabies, continental drinking habits; and foreigners would buy up mountain huts, lakes and forests' (ibid:33).

The Movement distributed leaflets, staged demonstrations, and used various symbols such as flags and traditional songs which added support to their slogan 'Defend national sovereignty' (Bjørklund 1997:149). Both the arguments and the symbolic materials used to support them were strong to catch the heart of the nation. Therefore, it was easy for the no-side to arouse the national identity dynamic against the EC-membership by strongly linking it to the national identity elements.

As a result, despite the overwhelming material resources which the yes-side was able to muster (the state apparatus, the major media, most major employees) the no-side won out. This result was important in two respects: it shows the people's capacity to organise themselves in opposition to the state, and it confirms that state did not have a monopoly on building institutions which embodied the nation and its will.

Result

The referendum on Norway's membership to the European Community took place on 24 and 25 September 1972. Of the 79.2% of the electorate who voted in the referendum 53.5% voted 'No' and 46.5% voted 'Yes'. Although the referendum was an advisory one, the Norwegian Parliament did not ratify Norway's accession to the EC, and Norway did not become a member of the EC.

The referendum result caused something like a political earthquake in Norway. The negative result meant the end of the Labour government, which had promised that it would resign in the event of a No-majority. A new centrist minority government, consisting of the newly split Liberal Party, the Christian Democrats and the Centre Party, took over on 12 October 1972. Norway signed a free trade agreement with the EC in April 1973, and this came into effect in July 1973. The individual agreements between EFTA countries and the EC secured the free trade and gradual elimination of tariff barriers between them. Agricultural products and fish were not included in these agreements.

4.4. Conclusive Remarks

Saeter (1996:135) argues that 'the 1972 EC-debate in Norway was probably the hardest fought political battle that has ever taken place in this country since the dissolution of the union with Sweden in 1905'. It had a profound impact on political life in Norway as a whole splitting political parties, organisations, institutions, groups and even families into opposing and often hostile camps.

The arguments in the 1972 EC-debate in Norway were very much linked to the national identity elements (see Table 1). The People's Movement, arguing against the membership, was successful in presenting how EC membership would not fit in with Norwegian history, culture, and identity. By using national symbols and the rhetoric of 1814, 1905, and 1940 it was successful in initiating the national identity dynamic by presenting the EC-membership as an equal threat to those in the history. Facing such a threat to its existence, national identity dynamic started to function and led 53.5% of the electorate to reject the EC-membership.

	Arguments	
	Yes-side	No-side
Fundamental Values	Norway and Europe shares the same culture	Hierarchical vs. egalitarian, centralised vs. dispersed, care about the strong vs. care about the weak, egalitarian peasant-based stock against European culture and its representatives
History	Colonial past is not negative	Critique of colonial past and neo-colonialism
Religion	Christianity as a common European heritage	Anti-Catholic feelings, Protestant Norwegian church vs. Catholic Europe
Union	EC as a community, solidarity, togetherness	Negative connotations of union with Denmark and Sweden
Sovereignty	Pooling of sovereignty in order to accomplish ultimate goals	Defence of self-government, EC will take away politicians' control over the economy
Agriculture and Fisheries	Growth in industry and trade	Agriculture and fisheries more related to culture and identity than money

Table 1: Arguments over the national identity elements in 1972 debate on EC-membership in Norway

The 1972 referendum result was not just an answer to the question on the ballot paper, but more a statement concerning what society desired for the future of their country. Sizeable groups of Norwegians felt their material and economic conditions threatened by EC membership, but more importantly, the concerns of these groups were shared by the large sections of the society due to these groups' being the core of the national identity. Here, agriculture and fisheries were about much more than simply money. It was the representation of Norway and the Norwegians. In order to underline this point, the opponents of membership often referred to the role of the Norwegian peasant in the nation-building process against the foreign-based elite and statesmen; and used the pictures of peasants and fishermen in the remote parts of the country standing by a small farm or a deep blue fjord in their propaganda materials. The success of the no side was to hinge the economics question solidly on the more basic question of sovereignty and demographics, that is, to an identity politics in favour of a certain idea of Norway, and a Norway which was superior to Europe.

By underlining concerns about sovereignty and the national identity, the no-side could successfully arouse the national identity dynamic. Nelson describes the anti-EC movement as 'an emotional appeal to the hearts of the Norwegian people. Europe was depicted as a menace. Good was struggling against evil' (quoted in Matlary 1993:49).

5. 1992 EEA Agreement and the Period of Adaptation

After the failure of the EC application, Saeter argues, the successor coalition government tried to restore the order and confidence in the Norwegian political system and to demonstrate towards the outside world that Norwegian foreign and security policy would remain stable (Saeter 1996:139). After the referendum all official discussion on the membership question was effectively stopped, and there was no pressure from outside to re-open the membership question. After all, even without membership everything in the country was going well, and the economy of the country was expanding. So, this 'climate of détente made a positive contribution to the policy of making membership a non-issue' (ibid:139).

Negotiations for a European Economic Area (EEA) started between EFTA and the EC in 1989 after a joint ministerial meeting. The EEA agreement offered access to the EC's internal market which was crucial to Norwegian industry (Sogner and Archer 1995:394), and was also useful to 'ease Norway into the EC through the EEA' (Archer and Sogner 1998:49). The aspiration was that the EEA agreement which could be completed by early 1991 would provide Norway and other EFTA countries the necessary adaptation to the EC's internal market and to the acquis communautaire.

Through the EEA Agreement, which was ratified on 16 October 1992 by the Storting, Norway committed itself to transpose most of the acquis communautaire related to the free movement of goods, capital, services and persons as well as the EU competition rules into its national legislation. The EEA-Agreement brought about an increase in cooperation also in fields like environmental protection, social dimension, consumer protection, research and development, education, training, culture, company law, measures for small and medium-sized enterprises, tourism, statistics, and information services. However, the Agreement did not include adherence to the common agricultural or fisheries policies, to the monetary policy, and the foreign and security policy.

6. 1994 Debate on EU Membership

6.1. Application Discussions

The hopes regarding Norway's apprenticeship in the EEA for some years were turned out to be vain with the unexpected applications of Sweden and Finland. The Swedish Social Democratic government suddenly decided to apply for membership and submitted an application in July 1991, and this was followed by a Finnish application. Thus, the situation for Norway was changed radically by Norway's two neutral Nordic neighbours seeking membership. As a consequence, by April 1992 Prime Minister Brundtland announced that it had been decided to submit a membership application to the EC, with the changes in Europe and the Swedish and Finnish applications being cited as reasons.

The Storting voted in favour of the membership application to be submitted on 19 November 1992 with a majority of 104 to 55. The opposition included 15 Labour representatives, 12 from the Christian Democrats, all of the Centre Party (11), and all of the Socialist Left Party (17). The remainder supported the application. According to the wording of the resolution, 'Norway should apply for membership under the pre-conditions that negotiations with the EC were to be concluded in parallel with those of other Nordic applicants and that the people through a referendum should be consulted on the outcome' (Saeter 1996:143). Therefore, the government delivered its application on 25 November 1992, and the negotiations started in May 1993.

6.2. Membership Negotiations

For the EU, Norway's application raised no political problems; free trade for industrial products had already been established between the two, and the EEA Agreement meant that Norway broadly accepted the acquis communautaire related to the free movement of capital, labour, goods and services. Also Norwegian accession was likely to strengthen the European Union in a number of policy areas such as democracy, low inflation, and environment. However, problem issues were regional policy, fisheries, agriculture, energy, state aid and state monopolies, alcohol restrictions, social policy, and trade policy. When applying for EU membership, Norway had to accept that transition periods would be given for sectors raising particular problems, but that there would be no permanent derogations. As a result, even during the preliminary negotiations, fish, petroleum, agriculture, and regional policy – as well as the broader sovereignty issue- were important to key sections of Norwegian public opinion (Archer and Sogner 1998:54). These policy areas had also significance for many as elements maintaining and protecting Norwegian national identity. For this reason, negotiations in key policy areas, i.e. fisheries, agriculture, energy, regional policy, are analysed in detail in this section in order to surface their linkage to the Norwegian national identity dynamic.

Fisheries:

In 1992, fish was the second most important of Norway's mainland exports with 90% of the total catch exported, 67% to the EU, of whose fish imports Norway supplied a quarter (Archer 1997:151). The Norwegian fisheries minister, Jan Henry T. Olsen, claimed from the outset of negotiations that the EU's fisheries policy turned him against Norwegian EU membership. He declared that Norway had no fish to give away and requested adjustments to the Common Fisheries Policy (CFP) (ibid:151).

Norway wished to keep its existing quota regime, and to maintain the strict enforcement of quotas and catching regulations. The government asserted that no new fishing rights in Norwegian waters could be granted to Communities' vessels, and requested unrestricted access to the EU for its fisheries products. Jan Henry Olsen, the fisheries minister, stated that Norway sought recognition of the dependence of its coastal settlements and fisheries resources, and asked to preserve its 12-mile exclusive fisheries zone at least until 2002. Norway also wanted to preserve its system of direct sales associations (Archer and Sogner 1998:64).

The negotiations on fisheries ended in March 1994. Although Norway accomplished two of its standpoints – to keep its 12-nautical mile exclusive fishing zone along its coast and to obtain duty-free access to EU markets for its seafood from the first day of its membership-, they had to exchange some fish, if not give away, in return of these demands. Besides, the right of management of the waters north of 62 degrees was to be transferred to the EU no later than 1 July 1998. From that date, the EU was to take over Norway's annual negotiations with Russia regarding the management of the 'grey zone' in the Barents Sea. Furthermore, Norwegian laws requiring Norwegian citizenship for the ownership of Norwegian registered fishing vessels were to be retained for only a three and a half-year transitional period, after which EU citizens would be able to purchase Norwegian boats. Lastly, EU market regulations for the sale of fish would replace Norwegian ones, and membership of the wholesalers' cooperative would no longer be compulsory. In the end, the final outcome of the negotiations on fisheries was interpreted as that 'Norway exchanged ultimate control over the regulation of its offshore fisheries – and a few extra cod- for freer access to a lucrative market' (ibid:65).

The immediate response of the fishermen's organizations was to reject the deal complaining about the loss of sovereignty over what they regarded as 'Norway's fish'. The 2,000 tonnes of additional fish which Mr. 'No-Fish' Olsen had conceded provoked anger (ibid:65).

On the other hand, the fish breeding industry was in favour of Norwegian EU membership. The sector was responsible for 30-40% of the income from Norwegian fish exports. They believed that 10,000-15,000 new jobs could be created in fish processing if Norway joined the EU (ibid:65).

Petroleum:

In 1972 Norway began the process towards becoming a major oil producer, and it was already clear that oil and gas would make a major contribution to the Norwegian economy. From the late 1970s, Norwegian oil and gas exports rose steadily, strengthening both the sector's influence in the Norwegian economy and Norway's position as energy supplier to Western Europe. The value of Norwegian oil and gas production in 1993 was around 1/7 of the country's GNP, while the sector made up of 1/3 of total exports. Nearly 90% of petroleum exports went to Western European countries (ibid:59).

The political principle followed in the petroleum sector had been to keep Norwegian sovereignty and national rights over resources, labelled as 'national guidance and control', which involves 'the administration of resources, national guidance of work on the continental shelf, the right to state participation, and the state's right to impose taxation and of ownership of petroleum resources'. The vehicle for this policy was the state oil company, Statoil, which held a 50% share of all licences (ibid:59). Norwegian government's position on energy was that 'it neither wished to rush into a change of conditions for off-shore production, nor wanted to be seen to alter its resources policy to come into line with EU policy which Norway had not helped to formulate' (Archer 1997:154).

However, in autumn 1991, the EC tabled a draft directive which proposed that EC companies could bid for off-shore resources on a non-discriminatory basis, regardless of nationality and of whether they were state-owned or private. This draft directive met with scepticism, and heavily criticised in Norway. As Western Europe's largest oil producer and as the third biggest supplier of gas to the EC, Norway was prepared to be assertive in relation to the energy sector. The trade minister Godal stressed Norway's favourable position, and portrayed Norway's membership as being of vital importance to the EU's future energy policy.

Important Norwegian demands were taken into account in the final text of the EC directive which was adopted by the EC energy ministers on 10 December 1993. The Protocol 4 of the Accession Treaty guaranteed Norwegian jurisdiction over its petroleum resources and recognized the right of state participation in the off-shore sector. The Protocol also confirmed national rights over the management of those resources which confirmed Statoil's position as an important political tool and as representing the state's continued direct involvement (Archer and Sogner 1998:61).

Agriculture:

Because of its geographical location, Norwegian agriculture has been made in the special arctic and sub-arctic climate, and for this reason farmers need special support from the state. Norway claimed that the EU should grant their agriculture a special Arctic and sub-Arctic status; and the climatic, topographical and demographic conditions of their country's agriculture should be compensated by guaranteeing Norwegian producers earnings similar to those farmers elsewhere in the EU (ibid:62).

As a result of the settlement, the EU's Common Agricultural Policy was to be extended to Norway with agricultural prices being adjusted to those of the EU from the first day of membership. Special measures could have been implemented during the first five years to prevent severe market disruption. The CAP's support policy was to be extended to the whole of north Norway and parts of the south. In these areas national support could not exceed the present level, and subsidies contrary to current CAP schemes were to be phased out over five years.

The settlement disappointed the farmers' representatives. Two main farmers' associations, i.e. the Farmers' Association and the Small Farmers' Association, and other relevant associations considered that it would be impossible to maintain Norwegian agriculture inside the EU which threatens Norway's distinctive nature (ibid:63).

Regional Policy:

Although EU's and Norway's regional policies were quite different, they both aimed at avoiding depopulation of outlying regions and encouraging development in rural areas. In the negotiations, the Norwegian government requested that all of Norway from Trondheim up to the Russian border should get EU support as especially underdeveloped regions. The issue of subsidies for Arctic and sub-Arctic farmers and for sparsely populated regions was met with understanding among EU officials, though it was pointed out that the GDP per capita in this region was not low enough to attract aid under Objective 1 of the Regional Policy (ibid:61).

In March 1994 Norway agreed with the EU that population density would be the criterion for regional aid under the Objective 6. The four northernmost countries – Finnmark, Troms, Nordland and Nord Trondelag- would receive about Nkr

0.5 bn yearly from EU funds, with the Norwegian government providing matching grants (ibid:62).

Result:

The success of the Norwegian membership negotiations were evaluated differently by proponents and opponents: 'Judged against what was expected by the government, the outcome was quite reasonable. There were some gaps in the fisheries settlement but the whole package probably represented as near as possible to a good deal. According to the opponents, however, the agreements both confirmed their worst fears and failed to ameliorate their causes for complaint: Control over fisheries was given away; agriculture and the regions were undermined; and even Norway's offshore oil and gas became subject to EU regulations' (ibid:66). They also opposed the outcomes of negotiations based on the opposition to the lifestyle represented by the EU 'something cosmopolitan, continental and unNorwegian' (ibid:68), and called for the protection of the core Norwegian values and traditions, i.e. 'the Norwegianness'.

6.3. Referendum Campaigns

Actors

By the time the government applied for membership, the 'No to the EU' campaign was already organized on a nation-wide basis. This was the basic advantage of the anti-EU campaign, because it did not wait for the formal outcome of the negotiations. However, the 'yes' campaign could not start their campaign until the terms of membership were known, which was March 1994 at the earliest. Secondly, while the 'no' groups were prepared to sink their differences in a common line against the EU, the 'yes' group, once initiated, was observed to be more fragmented and unclear about its message. The basic reason behind this fragmentation was that there was a deep and traditional political divide between the representatives of industry and commerce –and their parliamentary colleagues in the Conservative Party- and the Labour government.

There were many political and social organizations both in favour and against Norwegian EU-membership in the 1994 debate. To start with, the most important and biggest organisation opposing Norwegian membership of the EU was 'Nei til EU' (No to the EU) with 140,000 members which equals to 5% of the electorate nationwide, and up to 50% of the electorate in some small countryside communities (Seierstad 1997:7). In a small nation of four million, it was Norway's largest political organisation.

Under the leadership of Kristen Nygaard, a retired university professor, Nei til EU was organized as an ordinary political organisation: in each of 440 local municipalities local branches; in each of 19 counties a regional organisation with a regional congress every year electing a board and secretariat; and at national level a national board, an executive board and a national secretariat holding a national congress every year (ibid:7). There were also several subcommittees such as a women's committee, an EEA committee, and a youth branch 'Ungdom mot EU' (Youth Against the EU) (Archer and Sogner 1998:71). With a heavy campaigning from March 1991 onwards it arranged information meetings, and published leaflets, fact sheets, books, and newspapers.

Another no-group 'Social Democrats Against the EU' (SME) was established in October 1993 by influential Labour Party politicians, including former Cabinet minister Hallvard Bakke as the leader and another former minister Tove Strand Gerhardsen as the deputy leader (ibid:72). The SME stressed that it was not a faction within the Labour Party, but an independent organisation geared towards the referendum, after which it would disband.

In the spring of 1994 a closer cooperation established between Nei til EU, SME, Centre Party, Christian Democrats, Liberal Party, Red Electoral Alliance, Workers' Communist Party, Farmers' Association, Small Farmers' Association, and several youth and environmental organisations. A number of smaller or less serious organisations were also established such as 'Veterinary surgeons against the EU', 'The youth campaign against the EU', 'Hooligans against the EU', 'No for the sake of the EU', and 'Blondes against the EU' (ibid:73).

On the 'yes' side 'Europabevegelsen' (The European Movement) was the most important independent organisation under the leadership of the former rector of University of Oslo, Inge Lønning. With 35,000 members at its height in the autumn of 1994, however, it never became as strong as the Nei til EU (ibid:73).

The second organisation, 'Fra Nei til Ja' (From No to Yes), consisted of people who had changed their mind since 1972. Most cited the many changes that had occurred in Europe as the reason for their change of heart. Financial support came mainly from the employers' organisation and the Labour Party (ibid:74).

'Ja-aksjonen for norsk medlemskap i den europeiske union' (Action for Yes to the Norwegian membership of the EU) was established in February 1994 as a more outspoken group. It was headed by a former leader of the Labour Party's youth organisation, and was supported by a number of famous public figures. Archer and Sogner explain its aim as 'to create enthusiasm and self-confidence on the yes side, rather than to enter detailed discussions on the settlement'; and 'to make clear what would happen if Norway did not join the EU, and to show that this would mean a break with Norwegian traditions' (ibid:74).

Other organisations smaller in scope were established closer to the referendum, including 'Farmers for the EU', 'Women for the EU', 'Brunettes for the EU', and 'Lapps for the EU'. An organisation called 'Don't know' was also set up (ibid:74).

The EU-membership debate also split the traditional political blocs and created new political alliances in Norway. The Labour Party (with a voting strength 30-40%) was the most important actor, with all its resources, network and position in government. Gro Harlem Brundtland as prime minister, Thorbjørn Jagland as party leader, and Jens Stoltenberg as deputy leader, were the main actors in the government's campaign. The second biggest party, Conservatives (with a voting strength 20%) opted for yes, as did the Progress Party (with a voting strength 3-15%) which has racist inclinations. Three so-called 'centre parties' (with a combined voting strength of 20-30%) were against Norwegian EU-membership, and joined the ranks of 'no' campaign. The Socialist Left Party with voting strength of 6-8% and the ultra-left party, Red Electoral Alliance, with a voting strength of 1% were both opposed to membership.

Left	Centre	Right
Labour Party (+)	Centre Party (-)	Conservative Party (+)
Socialist Left Party (-)	Liberal Party (-)	Progress Party (+)
Red Electoral Alliance (-)	Christian Democratic Party (-)	

Table 2: Grouping of the Norwegian Political Parties Regarding the EU-Membership Question

Arguments

As was the case in all previous debates on Norway's critical decisions regarding its faith (debate on parliamentarianism in 1814, debate on independence from Sweden in 1905, liberation from German occupation in 1945, and debate on EC membership in 1972), the *functionalist* and *nationalist representations,* and their basic concepts were presented and fought once more in the debate on EU membership in 1994.

In order to clarify the wide-range of arguments of the Norwegian debate on EU-membership, this research classifies them into three categories as (1) political arguments, (2) social arguments, and (3) sectoral/economic arguments.

In the framework of the first category, i.e. political arguments, one can find the arguments on democracy, subsidiarity, and sovereignty which are all linked to the historical sequence of events of 1814, 1905, 1945. Since these elements are highly linked to the very existence of the Norwegian nation and the state, and they constitute significant elements of the Norwegian national identity, perception of them under threat would be a powerful factor mobilizing the national identity dynamic.

The second category, i.e. social arguments, is related more to the solidarity in the Norwegian society through employing a well-functioning and expensive welfare system and regional policy. These two policies also appear as indispensable parts of the Norwegian society since they provide the solidarity, equality and harmony in the society which are the proud elements that define and distinguish the Norwegian society. With such emotional and functional linkage, these features also constitute important and indispensable elements of the Norwegian national identity. Any threat to these elements (no matter it is a perceived threat or a real one) would mobilize the national identity dynamic.

Finally, in the third category, i.e. sectoral/economic arguments, one can find the primary sectors (agriculture, fisheries), the energy sector, and the related issues of national control and environment. These sectors (especially fisheries and energy) have a dual function in the Norwegian context: they do not only generate an enormous economic value as being the most important Norwegian exports and contributing highly to the GDP, they also have social and political consequences for Norway and therefore linked to the nation and society. It is only through maintaining and well-functioning of these sectors that economic consequences (revenues necessary to maintain an expensive universal welfare state – thereby solidarity, equality and harmony in the society-) and social consequences (scattered settlement pattern, populating the northernmost areas, and regional policy) required for the preservation and continuation of the distinctive 'Norwegian way of life' could be generated. For this reason, fear of losing national control on these sectors figured prominently in the EU debate by those who are opposed to EU-membership (Ingebritsen 1998:131).

To remind it again, the goal of the detailed analysis of EU-arguments (both positive and negative) is not to determine which of these arguments are right or wrong, but rather the actual aim of this analysis is to present (1) the close link between these arguments and the Norwegian identity elements, (2) how Norwegian identity elements were employed in the EU-discourses, (3) how these discourses influenced Norwegian people's perception of themselves and the EU, (4) how these perceptions led to the perception of a threat to the national identity elements, so led to the national identity dynamic to function, and finally (5) how the national identity dynamic in the Norwegian context influenced a major foreign policy choice (EU-membership). In this way, the clear demonstration of the sequence of the causal relationships from (2) to (5) will serve as an empirical validation of the social constructivist hypotheses.

1. Political Arguments

The most prominent argument on the No-side was that Norway is more democratic than the EU-system, and that EU-membership will have a negative impact on *Norwegian democracy*. On the other hand, the supporters of European integration argued the other way around, that EU is an 'additional democracy' that will contribute to the Norwegian democracy. This discussion, i.e. comparing different levels of democratisation and deciding on which side is right or better, is a highly normative task with no clear answer. Rather, for the aims of this research the significance of arguments on democracy is the linkage established between the democracy and the Norwegian national identity. Indeed this point was stressed by the No-side as that the Norwegian democracy has a firm rooting on early democratic traditions (see Chapter 3). They asserted that democracy is not only a form of government in Norway, rather it comprises social and economic democracy, and democratic principles underlying justice, education, culture. In this sense it has put its stamp on society for its being not solely a vehicle for the elite but its being based on the support of the people as a whole[19].

President of the Nei til EU, Prof. Kristen Nygaard explains the specificity of the Norwegian democratic tradition in these words:

> *'We have created a democracy in which we do not only elect representatives to send to far away power centres to decide for us. We have, by laws of local democracy dating back to 1837, left much of the power behind in the local societies (municipal units named 'kommune') where people live. In our country we know what it means to be governed from outside. We have had 400 years of union with Denmark and 90 with Sweden. In addition, we were occupied by the Nazis for 5 years. We know that we do best when we govern ourselves, and when we voluntarily cooperate with others on an equal basis. All these aspects of our society are in danger if we adopt the societal system and principles embedded in the Maastricht and Rome treaties. The member states of the EU are now all democracies, but the union they have created is not'* (Nygaard 1995:4).

As oppose to the Norwegian democracy tradition, the EU system was presented by focusing on its democratic deficit problem due to the lack of transparency, democratic legitimacy, and accountability. These problems were presented as the basic threats to the Norwegian democracy: The problem of transparency in the EU system was linked to the concern over the primacy of the participation and

---

19 In the Norwegian democracy, Rokkan argues, 'votes count in the choice of governing personnel but other resources decide the actual policies pursued by the authorities' (Rokkan 1966:106). This means that the crucial decisions on economic policy are rarely taken in the parties or in Parliament, rather the central area is the bargaining table where the government authorities meet directly with the trade union leaders, the representatives of the farmers, the smallholders, the fishermen, and the delegates of the Employers' Association. These yearly rounds of negotiations mean more in the lives of rank-and-file citizens than the formal elections.

representation rights of the Norwegian people in the system. The active role of all interest groups in the decision-making process in Norway dovetailed with the theme of how the EU reached decisions in back rooms, the implication being that Norwegian democracy had an open decision-making structure which enables representatives of all sections of the society and of different interest groups to have a say and to join in the mechanism.

To these criticisms, the EU-proponents argued that cooperation within the EU would be an extension of democracy beyond the borders of the nation-state. The Prime Minister, Gro Harlem Brundtland, identified the EU as an 'additional democracy' which would contribute to Norwegian democratic tradition. Among social democrats this was seen as a way of extending democratic control in areas where national democracy could not work (Sciarini and Listhaug 1997:420).

There was also a debate on *subsidiarity* which was centred on the idea that space and distance is important for democratic legitimization. The Yes-side attempted to base their arguments on that physical distance to decision-makers was less important in the jet age, and supported their position with a stress on EU's subsidiarity (or the closeness) principle. On the other hand, the No-side characterised Norway as the 'close to people democracy', and described Brussels as 'a distant and non-transparent centre' (Hille 2002:16). It was stressed that the strong relation between Norwegian state and society was based on the 'democratic state and society' (Norwegian 'samfunn') as a close unit, which was endangered by the EU-integration (Hille 2000:68-82). In the basic program of Nei til EU, it was argued, 'power should be there, where the people live' (Hille 2002:16).

In this subsidiarity debate ('distance to power'), there are two reflections of the centre/periphery: First, Norwegian rural periphery against the urban, power centre –Oslo; and second, Norway as the periphery of the EU. In order to understand the power of this argument, it is vital to understand the historical centre-periphery cleavage in the Norwegian context. Rokkan emphasizes that the real distances and remoteness of large parts of the country are relevant for this cleavage, but more striking is the Norwegian history, which is characterised by the struggle between countryside and centres of economic resources, political power, and the definition of leading culture. This also fits together with the observation of Norwegian scholars that the EU debate reanimated traditional cleavage-patterns between urban centre and rural periphery, which originated in the patterns of mobilisation of the last century (ibid:16).

The second dimension is about the setting of Norway in relation to 'continental Europe'. The presentation of Norway as a peripheral state of the European mainland and the promotion of a feeling of not-belonging to Europe are backed up by the geographical distance between Continental Europe and the High North, differences in history, and difference between the Catholic influenced continental

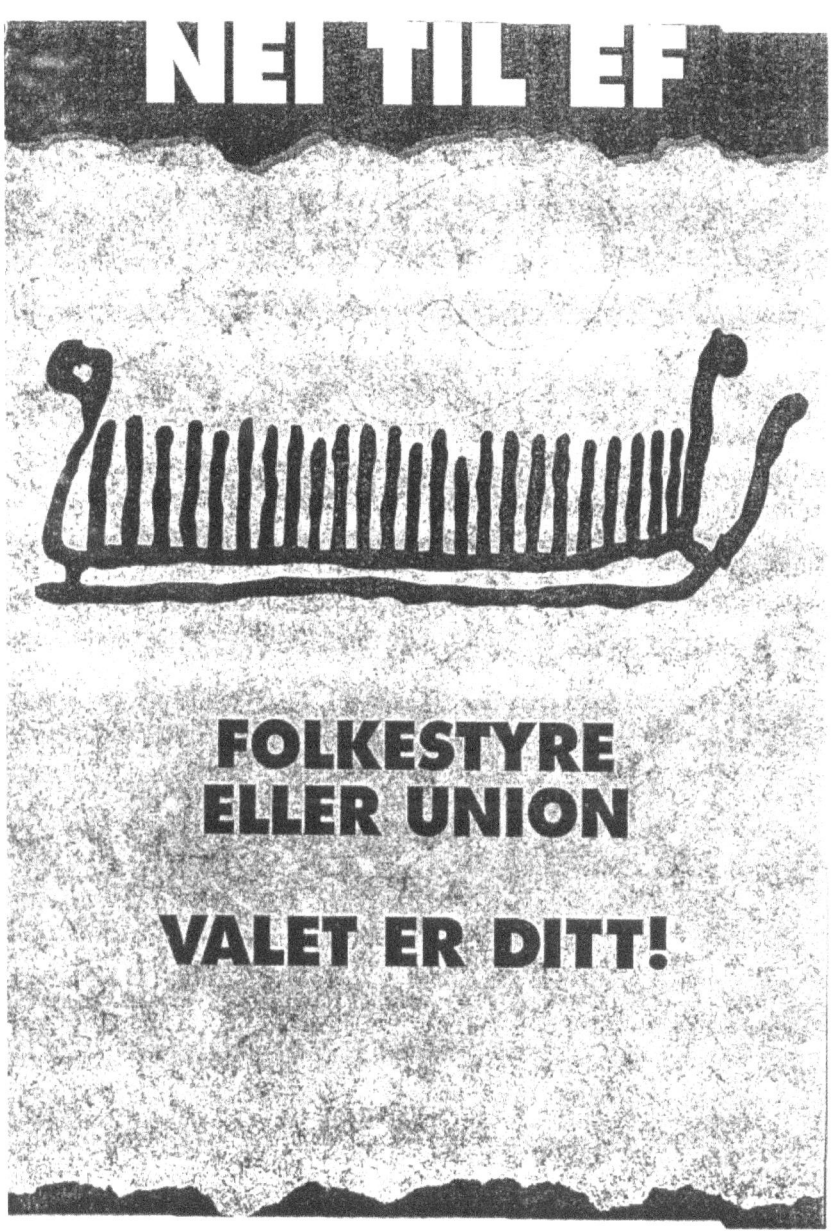

Picture 5: Self-Government or Union? Choice is Ours! –Campaign Brochure of the Nei til EU Movement

Europe and Lutheran traditions in northern Europe. Picture of Norway as a distant satellite of continental Europe regarding both the distance and the urbanisation was also employed: Europe was illustrated as the 'urban centre located in the south' and Norway was illustrated as the 'rural countryside located in the north'.

It is hard to say how valid these theories are to explain relations between Norway and the EU in the centre/periphery context; but the significance lies in the strategy of employing the centre-periphery argument at two levels in the 1994 EU-membership debate. In this argument, Europe is defined as the centre and Norway, and especially the peripheral parts of Northern Norway, as being at the outermost limits of the continent. These two levels of centre-peripheral relations or self-definitions are strongly intermingled. Such a definition brings about a Self/Other perception which also results in the mobilization of the national identity dynamic. This we can see in the popular slogan from the EU-debates of 1972 and 1994: 'It is a long way to Oslo, but even further to Brussels' ('Langt til Oslo, lenger til Brussels') (ibid:17).

The *loss of sovereignty* due to the precedence of the EU acquis communautaire over the Norwegian laws and decisions was another significant issue in the 1994 EU-membership debate. It was claimed by the No-side that: 'If we join the EU, all the EU laws, regulations and court rulings, the 'acquis communautaire', will have precedence before decisions in the Norwegian parliament, all Norwegian laws and even our constitution. This is a massive loss of sovereignty and independence' (Nygaard 1995:4). As opposed to that argument, the Yes-side stressed that Norway must join the EU in order 'to influence it, and to strengthen national sovereignty within the EU'. The Prime Minister argued that 'membership would provide Norway with a degree of national sovereignty far beyond that which it could obtain alone' (Archer and Sogner 1998:66). The EU-proponents also stressed the importance of the Nordic dimension in the EU by arguing that 'Nordic cooperation could flower inside the EU, but would wither if some Scandinavian countries joined and others did not' (Neumann 2002:121).

Moreover, a 'union' with European countries had overwhelmingly negative connotations in the Norwegian context reminding of the bad memories of imposed unions with Denmark, Sweden, and the brief occupation by Germany. The protection and maintenance of national independence and self-government were presented as significant counter-arguments to the European integration discourse. When the European Communities declared it as European Union it also triggered the negative connotations of 'union' in the Norwegian context, which strengthened the no-side.

In fact, the head of the European Movement declared that the game was over with this move:

'In the fight for the majority of the Norwegian people's votes, the game was actually up when the EC changed its name to the EU. That opened things up for the final brainwash, with the concept of the union as the detergent. For conspicuous historical reasons, it is easier in Norwegian than in any other language to use the word union in order to preclude any pretence to thinking, or remove any trace thereof' (quoted in Neumann 2002:123).

To sum up, negative connotations of the concept of 'union' were overwhelming, for reasons which had to do with the 'cultural' union with Denmark and the 'political' union with Sweden.

In the debate on the sovereignty issue, the No-side did not only present Norway (as a sovereign state) against the EU (as a union), but also 'people's rule' against 'state decisions'. This was the same cleavage we have seen through the Norwegian history. Indeed, Erik Solheim, leader of the Socialist Left Party, argued that:

'Historically, in Norway we have had political and economic elite which have been much weaker than in very many other places. We have no nobility in Norway. The civil servants (embedsmenn) received their political counter-thrust from a strong people's movement at the end of the last century, and during this century we have had strong people's movements which have dominated our country in opposition to the elite' (quoted in Neumann 2002:122).

Therefore, Nei til EU formed the slogan 'Yes to people's rule, no to the union'; and presented the dichotomy people/ state in tandem with the dichotomy Norway/ EU. Here the stress was first on 'the rule by the common people as oppose to the rule by the elite', and second, on the 'independent nation-state as oppose to a union' (ibid:121). Through Norwegian history in the 19th and 20th century, there has been a united Norwegian people, following the historical line from 1814, 1905 and 1945 by taking a stand for the independence against foreign dominion –whether it is Danish, Swedish or German; and this time in the context of the debate on Norway's EU-membership, the reference to these important historical events were explicitly employed by the EU-opponents.

The concept of 'the people' in this context was also tied with the 'Parliament' as the 'natural' sovereign locus of the state[20], and in this way it was the antithesis of the rest of the state and its European environment. The same representations are to be found in the events of 1814, 1905, 1945[21], and more recently of 1972. Thus, historical references to these events were rampant on the no-side in 1994.

On the pro-EU side, Labour's Foreign Minister, Tore Godal, commented on Nei til EU's arguments on democracy, sovereignty, and people's rule as such:

---

20 From 1814 to 1884, the split in the country involved the king, his bureaucracy and his government on the one hand, and Parliament on the other. Storting became the natural ally of the nation in the fight to do away with the foreign control.

21 See Chapter 3 for more detail.

Picture 6: It says 'We find ourselves in year 1994 after Christ. All Europe is conquered by Romans. All? No! A little foreign country resists. It is the struggled, stubborn people of Norway, of course. They will not bend. The way of living is comfortable. And the country cooperates and collaborates with most of the countries on the world, in an independent way, of course. For the Roman countries, like Germany, France, Belgium, the situation is not always simple. It seems to be an EU-period there'.

'I was left with the impression that the EU is a conspiracy to kill off people's democracy (folkestyret), the environment, equality, welfare and all the other things we cherish in Norway. But then I have a question: How come that some of Europe's oldest democracies have conspired to destroy everything that engages ordinary people throughout Europe?' (quoted in Neumann 2002:118).

The intention of this argument was to equalise Norwegian democracy with member country democracies, to reproduce the idea of 'the people' on the European level, and to move some of the emotional appeal of the idea of 'the people' away from the national level. By this way, the goal was to present that 'the people' is not an exclusively Norwegian phenomenon, but there exist other peoples in Europe as well who are as much tied with their states by dint of 'democracy' as the Norwegian people. Such a presentation was aimed to persuade Norwegian people to perceive themselves within 'the people of Europe' as one entity. Stoltenberg contributed to this presentation by arguing that 'Norway is a good place to live in, but this is due to Norway's already existing involvement in European cooperation' (quoted in Neumann 2002:118).

Therefore, 'democracy' and 'the people' cards were in use at both sides of the debate. This signifies the importance of both of these concepts in the Norwegian context and their relevance for the Norwegian national identity.

To summarize the political arguments, the arguments of democracy, subsidiarity, and sovereignty all point out to two dichotomies: (1) Norway (as a sovereign state) versus the EU (as a union hindering this sovereignty), and (2) the people (together with Parliament) versus the state (foreign-influenced bureaucrats). In Norwegian tradition, Parliament has always been 'the people's parliament', whereas the bureaucracy has been perceived as equal to the foreign control. Through the Norwegian history, both 'the people' and Norwegian Parliament, Storting, appeared as the champions of the national sovereignty and independence against the king, his bureaucracy and government; and therefore, became the most important elements of the Norwegian national identity. Mirroring the historical sequence of events, the argument 'the rule by the people against to be ruled by Brussels' was employed intentionally during the debate on Norway's EU-membership in order to refer to 'the dichotomies people/ bureaucracy, open/ closed, and centre/ periphery which were tied to the dichotomy Norway/ EU, where the former is privileged over the latter' (Neumann 2002:120). As a result, such arguments functioned strongly to mobilize the national identity dynamic by presenting (actual or perceived) threats to the crucial elements of the national identity.

2. Social Arguments

Solidarity was an important argument to attain the goal of preserving the national community as it was. National community in Norway is a dense and uncontested community, and is bound together by essentialist and nationalist ideas. The backbone of this national community was the solidarity, and this was obtained by the universal welfare system and the regional policy.

Norwegian welfare system is of the type 'universal model' from which all members of the society have the same rights and possibilities to benefit. This system has enjoyed an international reputation for combining generous welfare entitlements with rapid economic growth, low unemployment and very high levels of labour force participation, particularly among women. They appeared to have achieved the elusive combination of social equality and economic efficiency. Thanks to this system, when compared with the European countries, Norway is placed well ahead as regards the low unemployment and inflation rates and low ratio of the poor to the whole population.

Based on these grounds, the No-side argued that 'they will have a better chance of protecting the social solidarity outside the union' (Nygaard 1995:4), and strongly criticized the EU's social policy on three grounds:

First, 'within the union, there is, as a part of the general economic policy embedded in the Maastricht treaty, a definite preference for decreased public expenditures and increased privatisation – also in the welfare sector. The fear is that this policy will produce unemployment in Norway at levels approaching EU-levels. Wide-spread and long-term unemployment will in its turn weaken the solidarity and create increased social inequality and injustice' (ibid:4).

Secondly, 'the EU system required cutting off the subsidies to the peripheral regions after a period of transition, which means the demise of the peripheries and local societies. Even if the return of this population to these depopulated districts could be made possible after a couple of decades, they would meet a deteriorated infrastructure, and would suffer from the loss of very important 'tacit knowledge' accumulated about the use of the land and resources during the centuries of uninterrupted use and transfer of knowledge' (ibid:4).

Thirdly, 'the equality in the society, the life standards and the closeness between rich and poor would be deteriorated within the EU system due to the intervention of the capital/market forces into the Norwegian social democratic system and the transfer of the making of the legal regulations for labour to a supranational setting which is alien to the Norwegian national system (ibid:4).

The understanding of equality in Norway in comparison with that in the EU was presented by the leader of the Nei til EU movement, Kristen Nygaard, as such:

> *'Norway has tried to create justice and equality, but not only as an abstract human right, or not only relying upon the principle of 'everyone's right to become rich'. In Norwegian social security system people are not dependent upon their career in working life (not Bismark Model), but they have the rights because they belong in the society (the Universal*

Model). In the EU the number of people that are 'poor' according to the Eurostat definition is approx. 52 million, or about 16%. This figure has been increasing over the last couple of decades. In Norway the corresponding percentage is about 7%. Norwegians are very egalitarian in their political ideology, and this also is reflected in the actual income distribution' (ibid:3).

Dag Seierstad also criticized the EU's understanding of freedom and equality by arguing that 'the freedom of movement of capital and worker under the Rome and Maastricht treaties is only on paper – not in the real world':

'The owner of capital is free to move his capital whenever he is not content with the conditions offered him by the state, the local community or the workers. The worker is free to follow wherever capital settles – but only if he can bring with him his family and his local community and get rid of the debt of his house. Thus the balance is similar to the balance between rich and poor in Victor Hugo's Paris: They have the same freedom to sleep under the bridges of Paris' (Seierstad 1997:10).

A leading spokeswoman of the Socialist Left Party, Kristin Halvorsen, who was against joining the EU, also added that:

'Norway is one of the best countries of the world to live in. That is right, and not only because Norway is a rich country, but because we are the country in Europe where the differences between people are smallest, where we have built a system of welfare on the premise that the differences between people are small, with rights for everybody' (quoted in Neumann 2002:119).

These arguments were also supported by detailed statistics on the comparatively higher unemployment and inflation rates in the EU zone, and similarly higher ratios of the poor in European countries. As can be seen from the arguments, by the EU-opponents the EU system was perceived and presented as having a detrimental impact on the national assets as solidarity, equality, high living standards which are all maintained by the universal welfare system.

Another dimension, equality between men and women in the Norwegian society, was also added to this discussion. The EU was claimed by the opponents to threaten the position of women in the society: 'If Norway were to become a member of the EU, it would lead to Norwegian women losing the possibility they have today to influence the society they live in' (quoted in Neumann 2002:119). The idea here was that equality was everywhere in the Norwegian society, between regions, sexes, occupation groups; and it should be preserved for the successful continuation of the solidarity in the society.

In this context, the EU-opponents employed the concept 'we' and the undoubted superiority of the national values (solidarity, equality, democracy, welfare state, high living standard), and alienated the EU as the 'other'. Reference to these values was a good move to present Norwegian system as being better than that of the EU, which created a perception of 'we' the better and 'the other' not so good. Therefore, the dichotomy equality/inequality is successfully linked to the dichotomy Norway/EU. This perception was strengthened by the slogan 'Solidarity or (European) Union'. This slogan not only contributed to the perception of Norway and EU as radically different in terms of social values, but also created a threat to these important national values.

Another important feature of the Norwegian national community is the *scattered settlement pattern* which is maintained by a distinctive *regional policy*. The Norwegian regional policies aimed at enabling people to keep on living in the peripheries, with an infrastructure covering and linking together all populated areas in the country. The target of this policy, which has been implemented since the Second World War, is to prevent Norway from deteriorating into a few densely populated areas around the large cities, rather to maintain it as an interplay between vital local societies scattered over the country.

This choice was argued to be very different from that of most other countries, and different from the global tendency for increasing urbanisation. An indispensable goal of this policy was defined as 'there should be a fisher on each island and a farmer on each fjell'. Besides, the slogan of this policy 'City and country, hand in hand (By og land, hand i hand)' reflects the desire to equalise standard of living between rural and urban areas (Ingebritsen 1995:355). However, this goal could be achieved only through heavy state subsidies. Although these subsidies attained their goal of keeping the peripheries populated with equal living standards, they also made them dependent on state subsidies. Therefore, there were two different perceptions of this policy: On the one hand, public was largely in favour of the present system no matter how big the burden was, because it was seen as one of the means of protecting social solidarity in the society. This attitude was very well reflected in the work of the Nei til EU, which depicted the will of people not only to defend the welfare system, but also to 'keep peripheries alive' in order to preserve the national community as it was. On the other hand, the implied changes on this system due to the EU policies were long awaited excuse for the Norwegian government to get away from this heavy burden.

The issue of scattered settlement pattern brought the dichotomy centre/periphery linked to the Norway/EU. In this debate the High North was constructed as 'an antipode of an integrated Europe', and described as 'an alternative society to the central European society' (Hille 2002:5). The feelings of belonging to the North equalled with the name of the country (Norway means: 'way to the North'), and contributed to the perception/feeling of 'geographical distance from Europe' which is connected with the ideas of conflict between 'centre and periphery' (ibid:11).

The Government's ability to cope with these strong clashes between Norwegian and EU social systems as presented by the EU-opponents was weak. They could only give assurances that membership would not be a threat to Norwegian values. In this way they tried to calm down the anxieties of people by assuring them that the EU system would not harm Norway as argued by the EU-opponents. The Prime Minister Gro Harlem Brundtland argued that: 'In the European Union Norway could maintain its welfare system, settlement pattern, high employment and strong economic growth, without losing sovereignty' (Archer and Sogner 1998:69). Trade Minister Grete Knudsen added to that 'the agreement would secure Norway a good basis for developing its welfare society, securing high employment, strengthening environmental policy and working for European security wishes' (ibid:69). Fisheries Minister Jan Henry Olsen also noted that 'the settlement maintained Norwegian rights to fisheries resources wishes' (ibid:69). The Agriculture Minister Gunhild Øyangen stressed the importance of the permanent arrangements for Northern agriculture, and ensured 'it could still play an important role in employment and settlement over the whole country' (ibid:69).

However, such assurances were not as strong as the perceived (or real) treats implied by the EU system upon solidarity, equality, welfare system, and scattered settlement pattern which are perceived as the basic elements of the Norwegian national identity. Indeed, the no-side reinforced this threat perception by arguing that 'all these aspects of our society are in danger if we adopt the societal system and principles embedded in the Maastricht and Rome Treaties' (Seierstad 1997:10). It is not surprising that such a clear presentation of a threat to the basic elements of the national identity from its significant 'other' resulted in the mobilization of the national identity dynamic.

Added to these social arguments, there were also cultural and religious dimensions. Regarding the culture, it was argued, by joining the EU Norway would enter into a union with others who did not speak Norwegian, were not acquainted with the uniqueness of Norway's connection to the countryside and traditional values, nor would they be likely to conform to the 'norsk hver dag'. The romantic identification with rural traditions and nature was in sharp contrast to a more urbanized European society.

Furthermore, traditional Norwegian way of life has close ties to religion and morality since 'an indispensable part of the Norwegianness is Protestantism and cultural Puritanism' (Matlary 1993:45). For this reason, in the 1994 debate on EU-membership, religion constituted a considerable cut-off point from Europe[22].

---

22 The Reformation in Norway was imposed with a severe political hand, and all ties to European Christendom were eradicated with the abolition of monasticism and the expulsion of Catholics. This policy lasted until the mid-18th century when the laws on dissenters allowed for Catholics to enter the country and to gradually practice their religion. However, as a reminder of the severity of the Reformation in Norway one should keep in mind that Jesuits were allowed to reenter Norway only in 1965 (Matlary 1993:48).

Protestant church, deep moral values in the Norwegian society, and restrictions on alcohol and drugs were all perceived under the threat of the Catholic church and more liberal and free life style of European countries. Criticising the liberal and free life style of European countries, a later Minister and head of the Christian People's Party, Svarstad Haugland, argued that 'we have an EU internal market which among other things consists of the Netherlands and the union town of Maastricht, where narcotics are sold openly, we have Spain, with legalisation of hashish, we have the Minister of Trade's German sister party – the Social Democratic Party- which has the legalisation of hashish on its programme' (quoted in Neumann 2002:119). Even some fundamentalist groups compared the Union with the 'Beast of the Apocalypse', as described in the Bible, and strongly warned against joining (Pesonen et al. 1998:148).

There was no challenge from the EU-proponents to the No-side's representation of Norway, and an insistence that the EU is not a project of a kind with Norway. The only attempted challenge came from the Trade Minister, Grete Knudsen, who parodied the no-side for their giving 'the odd message: I am the best, look at me, learn from me! For I am the lighthouse!' (quoted in Neumann 2002:121).

To summarise, in the context of cultural and religious values, Norway and the EU were represented by the EU-opponents with dichotomies of healthy/sick, sound/ decadent and good/evil (Neumann 2002:119). In an overall analysis, presentation of Norway and the EU in the context of cultural and religious values resembled to that in the context of the welfare state, regional policy, solidarity and equality. In both cases the essence of Norwegian society was defined with its 'difference from Europe' (Wæver 1992:79), and was presented under threat by its 'other'. The other, that is the EU, was presented so controversial to basic Norwegian values and identity connotations that the final picture resembled to the Good against the Evil. This threat perception certainly triggered the national identity dynamic and called for a collective action of the Norwegian people to fight against the foreign influence/ or domination as they did in 1814, 1905, 1945, and more recently in 1972.

3. Sectoral/ Economic Arguments

Norwegian economy highly depends on the extraction, processing and export of oil, natural gas and related products. The importance of the Norwegian *energy sector* lies in that it generates not only an economic value, but also a social value: the income from oil and gas-related sources forms a significant part of the budget revenues which contributes to the resources available for public spending. So, the oil and gas revenue has become a way to support traditional sectors of the economy and enabled a substantial proportion of the population to remain in peripheral areas. It has been the Norwegian oil economy which subsidizes costly universal welfare system and social democratic policies untenable elsewhere in Europe. With such features energy sector is somehow linked to the Norwegian national identity.

Moreover, *primary sectors*, i.e. *agriculture and fisheries*, were also of great importance even in the petroleum age Norway, partly because they keep the rural areas populated (which is an important national policy), and partly because they have historical and emotional attachments originating from the Norwegian history. As discussed before, 'Norwegianness' was defined with a clear reference to the primary sectors, and farmers and fishermen were used as a symbol of the nation due to special historical and political conditions.

Historically, the *embedsmenn*, i.e. the Danish and later the Swedish King's representatives, constituted the urban power elite. As also local representatives in rural districts, they transposed Danish 'Europeanness' to the rural areas, but remained a foreign element as representatives of the Crown and as a power elite that was imposed. 'Norwegianness' was thus logically defined as a rural culture, closely identified with the farmer and the fishermen, as opposed to urban, 'imported' European mores (Matlary 1993:51).

Politically, the conflict over national identity was paralleled in the struggle for parliamentarism that ended with victory in 1884. Storting representatives from the periphery fought the Swedish King's representatives concentrated in Oslo, the *embedsmennstad*. Emerging victorious after a fifteen year's struggle, the rural representatives in Parliament, in the Venstre (Liberal) Party, celebrated the establishment of parliamentary democracy as the victory of 'Norwegianness' over foreign dominion (ibid:52).

Not surprisingly, agricultural, fisheries, and energy sectors were heavily involved in the 1994 EU-debate both on economic and social grounds. By using these sectors as national symbols the No-side gained a significant advantage in presenting their arguments that the EU-membership is incompatible with the Norwegian national interests and national identity.

In an emotional appeal to the Norwegian public, the Centre Party and the Nei til EU movement presented EU membership as a direct threat to farmers, fishermen and the traditional Norwegian way of life. With this aim, pictures of farmers and fishermen were used as the most popular motifs in publications and posters of Nei til EU. A good example of that is the usage of small fishing boats (quite typical northern Norwegian) in the propaganda material extensively (See Picture 7, 8, 9). They did not really indicate the actual number of people working on the boats and opposed to European integration; but the fishermen were used as a symbol for the national interest in general. Moreover, images of a lone Norwegian navigating an inland fjord, and a farmer standing beside his red-painted small cabin were also very popular motifs of the Nei til EU campaign.

Drawing attention to the dangers of the EU-membership for the Norwegian fisheries, the leader of the Nei til EU movement resembled the EU to the 'merchant kings' in the history:

> 'Once in time, there used to be 'merchant kings' along the coast who dictated fish prices and thus the living conditions for ordinary fishermen. The 'raw fish sales and distribution law' put an end to that. However, the EU system had negative implications on this protection of the Norwegian fishermen. Now our government is in the process of dismounting the law in order to 'harmonise' Norway to the spirit of the 'four freedoms', and we may once more get new 'merchant kings'; this time in terms of even more powerful foreign corporations' (Nygaard 1995:2).

There is an important point which needs to be underlined here: Farmers and farming do not have only a symbolic value as a national identity element in the Norwegian context, but also have a concrete value in Norwegian politics. In terms of electoral power, Norwegian farmers are overrepresented in national politics. In the Norwegian Constitution, a 'farmers' paragraph was included to protect rural interests by allocating seats according to a ratio of one urban seat in the parliament for every two rural seats (Ingebritsen 1995:353). By this way, farmers have been granted a disproportionate voice in Norwegian politics. Farmers have also played a critical role in the battle for parliamentarianism in the 1880s, and in the development of social democracy. This shows that the size of population sensitive to issues affecting farmers is far greater than those actually engaged in farming.

Employing the farmers and fishermen as the symbols of the nation, and the EU-membership as a direct threat to these symbols of the nation, the No-side mobilized the national identity dynamic. The success of this move was clear: Many Norwegians empathized with the position of the farmers and fishermen, and believed that they should be allowed to continue to engage in an activity which is closely tied to the history of the nation.

The *national control over natural resources* was another important issue in the EU-debate. The leader of the Nei til EU movement argued that: 'It is important for Norwegian people to safeguard their right to Norwegian resources, and Norway could keep better control of its own natural resources outside the union. Inside, Norway would have few means in securing national ownership' (Nygaard 1995:4). Maintaining national control and national policies over the natural resources were important in this regard, and the EU-membership was presented as a threat to both of them. To consolidate the threat perception, the EU-membership was resembled by the No-side to Norway's struggle for national control over natural resources in the 18th century:

> 'Norway is a small country with generous national resources. Around the turn of the last century, mighty neighbours from England, Germany and France wanted to take advantage of this situation and came to the point of buying up the exploitation rights to Norwegian natural re-

Picture 7: Yes to Self-Government – Campaign Brochure of the Nei til EU Movement

sources, waterfalls, forests, ores, which were the base for Norwegian industrial expansion in that century. Norway stopped that by introducing the 'concession laws', providing itself with the right to give preference to Norwegian interests. The law did not exclude foreign capital, but it required them to accept conditions regarding the mode of operation. Consequently, it became possible to build a Norwegian-owned industry and business' (Nygaard 1995:2).

To summarise, the No-side successfully presented the EU-membership as a threat to many national identity elements: political (democracy, sovereignty, people's rule), social (solidarity, equality, welfare system, regional policy), and economic/sectoral (agriculture, fisheries, energy sectors, and national control over natural resources). The emotional and historical ties to all these elements were still strong in the Norwegian society, so the No-side was extremely successful to win the hearts of the nation. The perception of a threat (no matter if it is real or perceived) to these 'indispensable parts of the Norwegian national identity' was another working strategy. Norwegian people want to maintain the Norwegianness for the years to come, and ready to struggle for that as their ancestors did in 1814, 1905, 1945, and 1972. Taken together, Nei til EU's discourses and presentations of self and the other resulted in the mobilization of the national identity dynamic in the 1994 EU-debate in Norway.

The EU-proponents had little to do against such a powerful mobilization. By appealing to an idea of Norwegianness, and representing the EU as a threat to society, the anti-EU movement placed the pro-integrationists on the defensive from the start of the campaign. So they have to defend why Norway should belong to the EU for a variety of economic and social reasons.

The Prime Minister Brundtland opened the government's yes campaign on 15 August 1994. Regarding the *foreign policy issues*, she, first of all, stressed the importance for Norway 'of being able to participate fully in the future development of Europe' (Archer and Sogner 1998:69). Then she stressed the security as a key reason for EU membership: 'Membership would secure the defence of Norway; the EU membership would give Norway, which shares a border with Russia, the safest basis for peace and security' (Brundtland, quoted in Archer and Sogner 1998:70). Third, she stressed the importance of the Nordic dimension, 'the importance of entering the EU side by side with the country's Nordic neighbours' (ibid:70).

When it comes to *domestic politics*, the Prime Minister stressed the positive impacts of the membership on Norwegian welfare and Norway's environment. She argued that 'the EU membership would strengthen the basis for environmentally friendly agriculture, as the area of Nordic agriculture recognised by the Commission could receive national support at the current levels' (ibid:70). Regarding the fisheries, she reiterated that 'Norway would retain the right to keep its 12-mile exclusive fisheries zone along its coast until 2003, when the EU Common Fisheries Policy would be reviewed', and maintained that 'this right could not be changed without Norway's consent' (ibid:70).

Picture 8: 'The Amsterdam-Pact: A tool for an increase in union development and Norwegian EU-membership' – Campaign Brochure of Nei til EU Movement

Bildnachweise:

det er tryggast
å seie nei!

Roma-avtalen «skal gjelde for uavgrensa tid» (§ 240).
Så lenge vi er usikre på kva konsekvensane av medlemskap kan bli,
vil vi på alle måtar vere best tente med å stå utanfor – som hittil.

Picture 9: *The Country Is Ours! Shout 'No'! It is safer to say no. The Rome-deal 'will last much longer'. As long as we are sure of the consequences of the membership, our country will stay out of it. – As we have done until now.-*

Yes-side also argued about the costs of non-membership. The main economic 'threat' was that 'the exports would be hit; the capital would move abroad and investments would decrease; the interest rate would rise; the value of the money, the krone, would drop; and the employment in industry would be hit' (Seierstad 1997:5). A leading spokesman of the pro-EU Conservative Party, Jan Petersen, argued that 'The heavy stagnation in the rate of investment in Switzerland after its no to the EEA demonstrates what kind of problems face countries which opt for isolation. A yes to Norwegian membership of the EU means a more secure future for Norwegian values (quoted in Neumann 2002:119). However, none of these arguments were catchy enough, since just after a year it was obvious that none of these expectations came true, on the contrary, 'the economic situation went even better' (Seierstad 1997:5).

Result

A very clever last strategy of the Yes-side was the employing of the so-called Domino-Strategy. According to this strategy the most pro-EU-countries would start the referendum vote (Austria and Finland), and they would be followed by the two unsure cases (Sweden and Norway). The idea was that the presumed positive vote of the 'safe' countries would bring the other countries into the EU (Jahn and Storsved 1995:21). The fear of the people that their country may become isolated in the new European order was at the centre of this campaign. However, this move met with strong criticism from the No-side. The leader of the Centre Party, Lahnstein, headed off the opposition in the following terms:

> *'The date for referendum was fixed by the yes parties who hoped that a Swedish 'yes' a fortnight earlier would create a so-called Swedosuction and influence people to do what the Swedes do. (Norwegian) people are hardly going to let themselves be coerced or threatened to vote in favour of yet again making Norway a part of a Union. And I think many balk at the thought that the Swedes are going to decide for us'* (quoted in Neumann 2002:117).

Before the start of the four referenda in sequence, Norwegian polls indicated 41% no, 46% yes, 13% undecided. On 12 June Austria voted for EU membership with 66.6% in favour. Four months later, on 16 October, Finland voted for EU membership with 56.9% in favour. These two positive results did not produce the positive momentum the yes-side had hoped for; rather it boosted the no-side in Norway. Immediately after the Finnish vote, polls indicated 51% no, 31% yes and 18% undecided. The polls showed that the majority of Norwegians were still sceptical about EU membership (Archer and Sogner 1998:76). One month later, on 13 November, the Swedish people said yes to the EU membership with 52.3% in favour. However, the 'Sweden effect' had lesser influence on Norwegian voters since 78% of the Norwegians said that they made their decision some time before the Swedish referendum (ibid:77).

Three days after the Swedish referendum Ivan Kristoffersen, the editor of Nordlys, recommended a no vote to his readers: 'We would be far from reality if we asked people to vote anything other than no. We would be extremely stupid to ask people to turn their back on their immediate environment, on the vulnerable ecology, and on the existing way of life for which Norway is responsible' (quoted in Archer and Sogner 1998:77).

Norway voted on the question of accession to the EU on 27 and 28 November 1994. The level of participation was unexpectedly high: 88.8%, the highest ever at any election since the introduction of the general right of vote in 1913 (Saeter 1996:144). It was also higher than the one in 1972 by 10%. The outcome of this advisory referendum, however, was not surprising to anyone. Of those voting, 52.3% said 'No' to membership, and 47.7% said 'Yes'. There had been a 0.6% swing to the 'Yes' side over a period of 22 years from 1972. The Prime Minister Brundtland accepted the result, and the Accession Treaty was never placed before the Storting.

6.4. Conclusive Remarks

In the 1994 debate on Norwegian EU membership, as it was in 1814, 1904, 1945, and in 1972, there was strong mobilization of the national identity dynamic. The result confirmed the power of the national identity elements to impact on the foreign policy decisions.

	Arguments	
	No-side	Yes-side
Democracy	Norwegian democracy was presented under threat by the EU's democratic deficit problem due to the lack of transparency, democratic legitimacy, and accountability	EU is an 'additional democracy' that will contribute to the Norwegian democracy, plus an aim to 'equalise' Norwegian democracy with member state democracies
Sovereignty	Joining the EU the 'acquis communautaire' would have precedence before decisions in the Norwegian parliament, all Norwegian laws and even our constitution which is a massive loss of sovereignty and independence	Norway must join the EU in order 'to influence it, and to strengthen national sovereignty within the EU'

Subsidiarity	Characterised Norway as a 'close to people democracy', and described Brussels as a 'distant and non-transparent centre'	Physical distance to decision-makers was less important in the jet age, and supported their position with a stress on the EU's subsidiarity principle
Presentation of Union	Negative connotations of the concept of 'union' were overwhelming, for reasons which had to do with the 'cultural' union with Denmark and the 'political' union with Sweden. Slogan: 'Yes to people's rule, no to the union'	Threats of 'isolation' by staying outside the union
Solidarity	Better chance of protecting the social solidarity outside the union	
Equality	Norway has tried to create justice and equality, but not only as an abstract human right, or not only relying upon the principle of 'everyone's right to become rich'. However, the EU's freedom of movement of capital and worker under the Rome and Maastricht treaties is only on paper – not in the real world'	Gave assurances that membership would not be a threat to Norwegian values.
Welfare State	In Norwegian social security system people are not dependent upon their career in working life (not Bismark Model), but they have the rights because they belong in the society (the Universal Model)	In the European Union Norway could maintain its welfare system, settlement pattern, high employment and strong economic growth
Regional Policy	The desire to equalise standard of living between rural and urban areas. Slogan: 'City and country, hand in hand'	The implied changes on this system due to the EU policies were long awaited excuse for the Norwegian government to get away from this heavy burden (state subsidies to regions)

Religion and Culture	Protestant church, deep moral values in the Norwegian society, and restrictions on alcohol and drugs were presented as under the threat of the Catholic church, and more liberal and free life style of European countries	No challenge. But parodied the no-side for their giving the odd message: 'I am the best, look at me, learn from me! – For I am the lighthouse!'
Agriculture and Fisheries	Presented EU membership as a direct threat to farmers, fishermen and the traditional Norwegian way of life. Used farmers and fishermen as the symbols of the nation	EU membership would strengthen the basis for environmentally friendly agriculture; Norway would retain the right to keep its 12-mile exclusive fisheries zone along its coast until 2003
National Control over Natural Resources	It is important for Norwegian people to safeguard their right to Norwegian resources, and Norway could keep better control of its own natural resources outside the union. Inside, Norway would have few means in securing national ownership	These rights could not be changed without Norway's consent

Table 3: Arguments over the national identity elements in 1994 debate on EU-membership in Norway

In the final analysis, the Yes-side was on the defensive from the start of the campaign. Against all national identity related arguments of the No-side, they had to defend why Norway should belong to the EU for a variety of economic and social reasons. However, these arguments did not succeed to assure the Norwegian people that their cherished values (solidarity, equality, welfare state) and national identity elements (farmers, fishermen, and scattered settlement pattern) would remain safe and untouched from the foreign influence.

The No-side used a clever double strategy, i.e. interest-related and identity-related arguments, in its campaign. *On the one hand*, they gave plenty of economic and political reasons why joining the EU would be disadvantageous for Norway. By establishing the EU in opposition to government by the people, solidarity, and environment, the No-side worked mainly to 'secure Norwegian sovereignty in areas vital to the Norwegian welfare state, to maintain solidarity with countries and groups of people dependent on financial aid, and to secure full freedom to administer resources and the environment responsibility' (from the Nei til EU bulletin, quoted in Archer and Sogner 1998:72). This argument first and foremost referred to the national interests, but all areas under consideration were also closely linked to the national identity elements. At the same time, by referring to the national interests, the EU-opponents responded to any accusation of being backward-minded nationalists in the periphery of Europe.

On the other hand, the No-side referred to emotions of people by employing discourses on the self and other. They used various national symbols such as Norwegian flags, traditional songs, fishing boats, Viking ships, farm houses, which added support to their slogans like 'The country is ours! Shout no!', 'Defend national sovereignty', 'Yes, we are many here in the North who can go better ways (than the EU)', and 'We do not want to be ruled from Brussels!' In these campaign materials, the EU was pictured as the other which is incompatible with the Norwegian nation. Indeed, the No-side defined the essence of Norwegianness with its 'difference from Europe' (Wæver 1992:79). They were enormously successful in presenting EU membership as a threat to core Norwegian values by using dichotomies of equality/inequality, healthy/sick, sound/decadent, people/bureaucracy, people/ state, open/closed, periphery/centre. These dichotomies represent the incompatible identity definitions of the two, and the perception of the EU as the other. The leader of Nei til EU persuasively argued that 'all these features relate to very fundamental characteristics of the Norwegian society, characteristics of which Norwegians pride themselves, and which they want to be strongly present in Norway also in the years to come' (Nygaard 1995:4). Indeed, the No-side persuasively argued with a common voice that 'their No implies a Yes to something better'.

Both of these strategies, i.e. referring to both the national interest and the national identity, provided the No-side both the rational and emotional underpinning. Social constructivist scholars assert that the social structure, interest, and identity are all mutually constitutive. Apparently, the Norwegian EU-opponents appreciated the social constructivist theory, and employed interest and identity elements grounded on the social structure in their campaign discourses.

As a result, the presentation of a threat (by the EU system) to the core values of the Norwegian national identity and interest contributed to the mobilisation of the national identity dynamic. The majority of the Norwegian electorate voted 'no' to the EU membership both in 1972 and in 1994 for almost the same reasons notwithstanding (1) the changing domestic and international environment in the 22 years period, and (2) the people's actual linkage to the elements of the national identity that are perceived under threat by the EU-membership. In other words, those who have only flimsy ties to agriculture, fisheries, and rural areas supported the interests of these groups and voted no. This behaviour can only be explained by the emotional value of these national identity elements for the wider sections of the society.

In both EU-debates in Norway, the No-side: (1) employed arguments closely related to the national interest and identity elements, (2) presented the EU as a threat to Norwegian identity elements, (3) mobilised the national identity dynamic, and finally (4) led the Norwegian people to vote no to the EU-membership. This sequence of events empirically validates the social constructivist hypotheses.

Chapter 5: Conclusion

This book aims to explain Norwegian people's reluctance to join the European integration. The rejection of the EU-membership in 1972 and 1994 with a consistent majority is interesting because although the international and domestic environments have changed considerably, Norwegian referendum debates and results have remained the same.

The explanations for this foreign policy choice vary widely among scholars. To start with, Rokkan (1966, 1967) referred to the cleavages in the Norwegian society on the territorial-cultural dimension (centre-periphery) and on the economic-functional dimension (producers such as farmers and fishermen and the consumers) (employers and employees) composing the two sides of the society. Valen (1981) stressed that the 1972 and 1994 referenda were characterized by all these cleavages being activated. While this explanation is able to pinpoint the pattern of behaviour, it does not shed light on the question of motivation.

Bjørklund (1997) analyzed the results of the 1972 and 1994 referenda according to five different perspectives: (1)interest explanations, (2)cultural explanations, (3)opposing the elite/government, (4)generation perspective, (5)cleavage model. Among them, he stressed the interest explanations and interpretations based upon differences in culture, values and norms. However, he argued that 'it is difficult to differentiate the two, and draw clear-cut conclusions' (Bjørklund 1997:154).

Ingebritsen (1995, 1997) employed a 'political economy based sectoral approach' and focused on the role of the leading sector (petroleum) and secondary sectors (agriculture and fisheries) in generating the negative result in the EU-referenda. She put forward that these leading sectors' political representation and influence on the country's elite were strong enough to exert pressure on the decision over EU membership. However, this explanation almost seem to suggest that the political leaders of the country are the pawns of the leading sectors and play only a marginal role in the decision on EU membership. Moreover, only a small and shrinking percentage of Norwegians are involved in the primary economic sectors of fishery and agriculture.

Neumann (2002) moved beyond rationalist premises and employing the identity politics. He presented the No-side 'not as aggregations of individual rational interests, but as instantations of identity politics' (Neumann 2002:89). Aardal (1994) also stressed the difference between EU and Norwegian values which have central importance in Norwegian political history and cultural life producing cleavages between Norway and the EU in similar lines with cleavages between centre versus periphery, rural versus urban, primary versus processing industries, national versus foreign/supranational government, welfare state versus free market liberalism (Aardal 1994:7).

However, none of these explanations offers a mechanism to link the national identity and the foreign policy decisions. This is exactly where most social constructivist scholars are criticized: 'they fail to provide concrete and testable causal mechanisms through which the process of choosing policies and defining interests takes place' (Moravcsik 1999:671).

In order to offer a testable causal mechanism between the national identity definitions and the foreign policy decisions, this book employed the *middle-ground social constructivist approach*[23], which explains the impact of the identities and interests on the foreign policy choices, together with the *individual psychology approach*, i.e. the 'national identity dynamic'[24], which seeks to answer questions as 'Why large groups of people act together in certain political situations?', 'How do masses mobilize for or against certain foreign policy decisions?', 'Is there a method for explicating the relationship between the mass attitudes and actual foreign policy decisions?'.

This book put forward five main theoretical hypotheses:

(1) National identities are not things we are born with, but are formed and transformed within and in relation to representation. National cultures construct identities by producing meanings about 'the nation' with which we can identify; these are contained in the stories which are told about it, memories which connect its present with its past, and images which are constructed of it (Hall 1992:292-293).

(2) National identity is constructed by means of 5 elements: (1) narrative of nation as a set of stories, images, landscapes, scenarios, historical events, national symbols and rituals which stand for, or represent, the shared experiences, sorrows, and triumphs and disasters which give meaning to the nation; (2) emphasis on the common homeland or territory signifying the origins, continuity, tradition, and timelessness; (3) the invention of traditions which seek to inculcate certain values and norms of behaviours by repetition

---

23 See Marcussen et al. 1999, 2001; Marcussen 2005.
24 See Bloom 1993.

which automatically implies continuity with a suitable historical past; (4) the foundational myth which is a story which locates the origin of the nation, the people and their national character so early that they are lost in the mists of, not real, but mythic time; (5) the idea of a pure, original people or 'folk'.

(3) The construction of the national identity takes place through classificational systems inscribed in law, through bureaucratic procedures, educational structures and social rituals, by means of which the state contributes to the construction of what is commonly designated as national identity (Bourdieu 1994:7).

(4) The power of the national identity lies in its ability to produce both political integration and national mobilization. National identity describes (1) the condition in which a mass of people have made the same identification with national symbols –have internalized the symbols of the nation-, and (2) the possible mass mobilization of this people to act as one psychological group when there is a threat to, or the possibility of enhancement of, the symbols of national identity (Bloom 1990:52).

(5) An analysis of foreign policy choices does not imply an analysis of material facts only, but also the human interpretation (social construction) of these material conditions in any national context. For this reason, this book is concerned with the perception of Norwegian people of themselves and of the EU, and their perception of interests and threats associated with the EU-membership[25].

The condition for the mobilization of the national identity dynamic is that images and experiences concerning international events or foreign policy decisions are presented to the mass public in such a way that either national identity is perceived to be threatened, or the opportunity is present to enhance national identity. Then the identification imperative will tend to work through the mass public as a national whole. Under the circumstances of either a threat or the possibility of enhancement, the mass national public as one group will seek to secure, protect and enhance their general national identity. The national identity dynamic, therefore, describes the social-psychological dynamic by which a mass national public may be mobilized in relation to its international environment. This, claims Bloom, is to state explicitly that the mass national public has a clear and psychologically coherent relationship with international affairs: 'The mass national public will mobilize when it perceives either that national identity is threatened, or that there is the opportunity of enhancing national identity' (Bloom 1990:79).

---

25 This study is not concerned with the actual facts about the EU, i.e. what the European supranational identity actually is, what effects it has on the national identities, whether it is really a threat to national systems; rather it solely focuses on the Norwegian people's perceptions and ideas about themselves and the EU.

To summarise, the mechanism between the national identity definitions and the concrete foreign policy decisions is the national identity dynamic. This mechanism helps to explain which ideas and discourses influence which policies under which circumstances. So, this book offers a testable causal mechanism between the national identity definitions and the foreign policy decisions. This mechanism is employed to Norway as a case study here.

Building on these theoretical grounds, Chapter 3 analyzed the 'construction' of the Norwegian national identity in the 19th century, and Chapter 4 analyzed the 'functioning' of the Norwegian national identity dynamic in the EU-debates in 1972 and 1994. The causal linkage between these two chapters is that while the former depicts the defining elements of the Norwegian national identity through 'invention' and 'internalization' of the symbols of the nation, the latter demonstrates the perception/ presentation of threat, that is the EC/EU, to these national symbols, and the mobilization of the national identity dynamic.

In Chapter 3, five fundamental composing elements of the national identity were presented as:

(1) the history composed of struggles for independence (from imposed unions with Denmark and Sweden) and for people's rule (against to be ruled by the foreign elite);
(2) the adventurous, glorious, warrior Vikings as the foundational myth;
(3) a beautiful homeland in the North where the land and the sea are tied strongly against the urban cities;
(4) idea of people living a simple and dour life in freedom (against the Danish-influenced urban civil servant stratum);
(5) the farmer (who joined forces with the national parliament in the struggle for independence) as the national hero.

The art, music, literature and public ceremonies played an important role in consolidating these national symbols to generate national sentiments into all people.

On this background, Chapter 4 analyzed the second part of this theoretical assumption, namely the functioning of the 'national identity dynamic'. Throughout this chapter, views and perceptions of the Norwegian people about themselves and Europe, and how compatible or conflictive are these perceptions are presented and discussed[26]. This analysis revealed that both in 1972 and 1994 EU-debates in Norway, arguments fell into three categories as (1) political arguments, (2) social arguments, and (3) sectoral/economic arguments.

---

26 This study is not concerned with the actual facts about the EU, i.e. what the European supranational identity actually is, what effects it has on the national identities, whether it is really a threat to national systems; rather it solely focuses on the Norwegian people's perceptions and ideas about themselves and the EU.

In the framework of the first category, i.e. political arguments, we found the arguments on democracy, subsidiarity, and sovereignty which are all linked to the historical sequence of events of 1814, 1905, 1945[27]. Since these elements are highly linked to the very existence of the Norwegian nation and the state, and they constitute significant elements of the Norwegian national identity, perception of them under threat was a powerful factor mobilizing the national identity dynamic.

The second category, i.e. social arguments, is related to the solidarity, equality, scattered settlement pattern, which are maintained by a well-functioning and expensive welfare system and regional policy. So, these policies gained an emotional and functional linkage to the Norwegian national identity as the providers of the proud elements that define and distinguish the Norwegian society. Different welfare and regional policies of the EU posed a threat to these elements and mobilized the national identity dynamic.

In the third category, i.e. sectoral/economic arguments, we found the primary sectors (agriculture, fisheries), the energy sector, and the national control over natural resources. These sectors (especially fisheries and energy) provide both economic consequences (revenues necessary to maintain an expensive universal welfare state – thereby solidarity, equality and harmony in the society-) and social consequences (scattered settlement pattern, populating the northernmost areas, and regional policy) required for the preservation and continuation of the distinctive 'Norwegian way of life'. Farmers and farming were used extensively as national symbols because of their symbolic value as a national identity element in the Norwegian context because of their critical role in the battle for parliamentarianism in the 1880s and in the development of social democracy. For this reason, fear of losing national control on all these sectors (agriculture, fisheries, energy) figured prominently in the EU debate and the presentation of the EU-membership as a direct threat to these symbols of the nation mobilized the national identity dynamic.

The aim of this discourse analysis was to present:

(1) how Norwegian identity elements were employed in the EU-discourses,
(2) how these discourses influenced Norwegian people's perception of themselves and EU,
(3) how these perceptions led to the perception of a threat to the national identity

---

27   In 1814, 1905 and 1945 there were a united Norwegian people taking a resolute stand for the independence against foreign dominion –whether it is Danish, Swedish or German. In Norwegian history (before the EU-debates) three instances of the functioning of national identity dynamic can be observed: at the time of declaration of Norway independent of Danish rule in 1814, at the time of dissolving the imposed union with Sweden in 1905, and finally at the time of resistance to the German occupation in 1945.

elements, so led to the national identity dynamic to function,
(4) how the national identity dynamic in the Norwegian context influenced a major foreign policy choice (EU-membership).

In both EU-debates in Norway, the No-side referred to emotions of people by employing discourses on self and other. They used various national symbols such as Norwegian flags, traditional songs, fishing boats, Viking ships, farm houses, which added support to their slogans like 'The country is ours! Shout no!', 'Defend national sovereignty', 'Yes, we are many here in the North who can go better ways (than the EU)', and 'We do not want to be ruled from Brussels!' In these campaign materials, the EU was pictured as the other which is incompatible with the Norwegian nation.

Indeed, the No-side defined the essence of Norwegianness with its 'difference from Europe' (Wæver 1992:79). They were enormously successful in presenting EU membership as a threat to core Norwegian values by using dichotomies of equality/inequality, healthy/sick, sound/decadent, people/bureaucracy, people/state, open/closed, periphery/centre. These dichotomies represent the incompatible identity definitions of the two, and the perception of the EU as the other. The leader of Nei til EU persuasively argued that 'all these features relate to very fundamental characteristics of the Norwegian society, characteristics of which Norwegians pride themselves, and which they want to be strongly present in Norway also in the years to come' (Nygaard 1995:4). Indeed, the No-side persuasively argued with a common voice that 'their No implies a Yes to something better'.

This analysis revealed that in both EU-debates in Norway the No-side:

(1) employed arguments closely related to the national interest and identity elements,
(2) presented the EU as a threat to Norwegian identity elements,
(3) mobilized the national identity dynamic,
(4) led the Norwegian people to vote no to the EU-membership.

This sequence of events confirmed and empirically validated the theoretical hypotheses of this research.

This study contributed to the existing literature in at least 4 ways:

(1) It answered 'How Norwegian national identity was constructed in the 19th century by the Norwegian national elite?' The answers provided to this question also confirmed Hobsbawn's *theory of nationalism*. Hobsbawn's 'invented traditions' means 'a set of practices, normally governed by overtly or tacitly accepted rules and of a ritual or symbolic nature, which seek to inculcate certain values and norms of behaviour by repetition, which automatically

implies continuity with the past' (Hobsbawn and Ranger 1983:1).
(2) It answered 'Did Norwegian national identity influenced the foreign policy decision about EU-membership?' The answers provided to this question confirmed the *social constructivist theory* that actors' behaviours (actions) are determined by their ideas and identities which are in a mutual relationship with immediate structural constraints (norms).
(3) It answered 'How ideas and identities impact on foreign policy decisions?' and 'What is the causal mechanism between national identities and the foreign policy decisions?' The answers provided to this question confirmed the *national identity dynamic approach* as the intervening mechanism. According to this approach, the mass national public will mobilize when it perceives either that national identity is threatened, or that there is the opportunity of enhancing national identity (Bloom 1993:79).
(4) Finally, it addressed the criticism of the social constructivist approaches that they offer few testable hypotheses and no causal mechanisms. As an answer to such criticisms this book offered the national identity dynamic as the causal mechanism which enables the researchers to test the 'power' of national identity in any national context.

The theory and the empirical methodology employed in this book can be applied to other national contexts. By this way, this book offers an interesting avenue for future researches on other countries' relations with the EU.

Bibliography

Allardt, Erik; Andren, Nils; Friis, Erik J.; Gislason, Gylfi P.; Nilson, Sten Sparre; Valen, Henry; Wendt, Frantz; Wisti, Folmer (1981) (eds.) *Nordic Democracy – Ideas, Issues and Institutions in Political, Economic, Educational, Social and Cultural Affairs of Denmark, Finland, Iceland, Norway and Sweden-*, Copenhagen: Det Danske Selskab

Andersen, Svein (2000) *Norway: Insider and Outsider*, Oslo: ARENA Working Paper, No.4

Andreas, Føllesdal (2001) *Citizenship: European and Global*, Oslo: ARENA Working Paper, No.22

Angell, Svein Ivar (1999) 'Some Reflections on National Identity in Norway and Sweden' in Barth, Theodor and Enzell, Magnus (eds.) *Collective Identity and Citizenship in Europe – Fields of Access and Exclusion –*, Oslo: ARENA/ The Van Leer Institute Report, No.3

Anttonen, Pertti J. (1996) (ed.) *Making Europe in Nordic Contexts*, Jyväskylä: NIF Publications

Arbman, Holger (1969) *The Vikings*, London and New York: Praeger

Archer, Clive (1997) 'Norway: The One That Got Away' in Redmond, John (ed.) *The 1995 Enlargement of the European Union*, Aldershot: Burlington: Singapore: Sydney: Ashgate

Archer, Clive and Sogner, Ingrid (1998) *Norway, European Integration and Atlantic Security*, London: New Delhi: Thousand Oaks: Sage Publications

Arter, David (1999) *Scandinavian Politics Today*, Manchester and New York: Manchester University Press

Arter, David (1984) *The Nordic Parliaments – A Comparative Analysis –*, New York: St.Martin's Press

Bakke, Elisabeth (1995) *Towards a European Identity?*, Oslo: ARENA Working Paper, No.10

Barth, Theodor and Enzell, Magnus (1999) (eds.) *Collective Identity and Citizenship in Europe – Fields of Access and Exclusion –*, Oslo: ARENA/ The Van Leer Institute Report, No.3

Beate, Huseby and Listhaug, Ola (1995) 'Identifications of Norway with Europe: The Impact of Values and Centre-Periphery Factors' in de Moor, Ruud (ed.) *Values in Western Societies*, Tilburg: Tilburg University Press

Berman, Patricia G. (1997) 'Edvard Munch's Peasants and the Invention of Norwegian Culture' in Brown, Berit (ed.) *Nordic Experiences –Exploration of Scandinavian Cultures*, Westport, Connecticut, London: Greenwood Press

Bjørklund, Tor (1997) 'Old and New Patterns: The 'No' Majority in 1972 and 1994 EC/EU Referendums in Norway', *Acta Sociologica*, Vol.40, No.2, pp.143–159

Bjørklund, Tor (1996) 'The Three Nordic 1994 Referenda Concerning Membership in the EU', *Cooperation and Conflict*, Vol.31, No.1, pp.11–37

Bloom, William (1990) *Personal Identity, National Identity and International Relations*, Cambridge: Cambridge University Press

Brown, Berit (ed.) (1997) *Nordic Experiences –Exploration of Scandinavian Cultures*, Westport, Connecticut, London: Greenwood Press

Brøndsted, Johannes (1960) *The Vikings*, Penguin Books: London and New York

Burgess, J. Peter (1999) 'The Logic of Language and Nation in the Emergence of Nynorsk' in Barth, Theodor and Enzell, Magnus (eds.) *Collective Identity and Citizenship in Europe – Fields of Access and Exclusion –*, Oslo: ARENA/ The Van Leer Institute Report, No.3

Claes, Dag Harald and Fossum, John Erik (2002) *Norway, The EEA and Neo-Liberal Globalism*, Oslo: ARENA Working Paper, No.29

Cohat, Y. (1992) *The Vikings – Lords of the Seas –*, London: Thames and Hudson

Cole, John and Cole, Francis (1993) *The Geography of the European Community*, London: New York: Routledge

Connery, Donald S. (1966) *The Scandinavians*, London: Eyre and Spottiswoode

Curtis, Michael (1965) *Western European Integration*, New York: Harper&Row

Dagre, Tor (1996) 'The History of Norway', produced for the Ministry of Foreign Affairs by Nytt fra Norge, Source: http://www.cyberclip.com/Katrine/NorwayInfo2/Articles/HistNorw.html, accessed on April 20, 2010.

Damgaard, Erik et al. (ed.s) (1992) *Parliamentary Change in the Nordic Countries*, Oslo: Scandinavian University Press

Derry, T.K. (1979) *A History of Scandinavia*, University of Minnesota Press: Minneapolis

Diez, Thomas (2001) 'Europe as a Discursive Battleground', *Cooperation and Conflict*, Vol.36, No.1, pp. 5–39

Dinan, Desmond (1999) *Ever Closer Union: An Introduction to European Integration*, London: Macmillan

Eide, Espen Barth (1996) 'Adjustment Strategy of a Non-Member: Norwegian Foreign and Security Policy in the Shadow of the EU', *Cooperation and Conflict*, Vol.31, No.1, pp.69-105

Einhorn, Eric and Logue, John (1989) *Modern Welfare States – Politics and Policies in Social Democratic Scandinavia –*, New York: Praeger

Elder, Neil, Thomas, Alastair, Arter, David (1988) *The Consensual Democracies? – The Government and Politics of the Scandinavian States –*, Oxford and New York: Basil Blackwell

Eriksen, Thomas Hylland (1996) 'Norwegians and Nature', Source: http://www.cyberclip.com/Katrine/NorwayInfo/Articles/Norw&Nature.html, accessed on April 20, 2010.

Finnemore, Martha (1996) *National Interests in International Society*, Ithaca and London: Cornell University Press

Fitzhugh, William and Ward, Elisabeth (ed.s) (2000) *Vikings – The North Atlantic Saga –*, Washington and London: Smithsonian Institution Press

Fossum, John Erik (2001) *Identity-Politics in the European Union*, Oslo: ARENA Working Paper, No.17

Fossum, John Erik and Eriksen, E.O. (1999) *Democracy in the European Union*, Oslo: ARENA Working Paper

Fulsås, Narve (2000) 'Norway: The Strength of National History' in Frank Meyer and Jan Eivind Myhre (ed.s) *Nordic Historiography in the 20th Century*, Oslo: University of Oslo

Gerhardsen, Tove Strand (1994) *Social Democratic Alternative*, Oslo: Scandinavian University Press

Geyer, Robert, Ingebritsen, Christine, Moses, Jonathon (ed.s) (2000) *Globalization, Europeanization and the End of the Scandinavian Social Democracy?*, Palgrave: New York

Graham-Campbell, James (2001) *The Viking World*, Francis Lincoln Publishers

Granell, Francisco (1997) 'The First Enlargement Negotiations of the EU' in Redmond, John (ed.) *The 1995 Enlargement of the European Union*, Aldershot: Burlington: Singapore: Sydney: Ashgate

Granell, Francisco (1995) 'The European Union's Enlargement Negotiations with Austria, Finland, Norway and Sweden', *Journal of Common Market Studies*, Vol.33, No.1, pp.117–139

Grell, Ole Peter (1995) *The Scandinavian Reformation – From Evangelical Movement to Institutionalization of Reform –*, Cambridge University Press: Cambridge and New York

Griffiths, Richard T. and Pharo, Helge Ø. (1995) *Small States and European Integration – Literature Survey and Evaluation –*, Oslo: ARENA Working Paper, No. 19

Grimley, Daniel M. (2006) *Grieg: Music, Landscape and Norwegian Identity*, The Boydell Press

Grindheim, Jan Erik (2002) 'Norway, Switzerland and the EU: Going Steady or Just Good Friends?' in Moxon-Browne, Edward (ed.) *EU and the CFSP*, Centre for European Studies, University of Limerick

Heisler, Martin O. (1990) (ed.) *The Annals of the American Academy of Political and Social Science 'The Nordic Region: Changing Perspectives in International Relations'*, Newbury Park: London: New Delhi: Sage Publications

Hemmer, Bjørn (1996) 'The Dramatist Henrik Ibsen', Source: http://www.cyberclip.com/Katrine/NorwayInfo/Articles/Ibsen.html, accessed on April 20, 2010.

Hille, Jochen (2002) Unpublished essay *'The Northern Antipode to European Integration'*.

Høifødt, Frank (1996) 'Edvard Munch', Source: http://www.cyberclip.com/Katrine/NorwayInfo/Articles/Munch.html, accessed on April 20, 2010.

Huseby, Beate and Listhaug, Ola (1995) 'Identification of Norwegians with Europe: The Impact of Values and Centre-Periphery Factors' in de Moor Ruud (ed.) *Values in Western Societies,* Tilburg: Tilburg University Press

Ingebritsen, Christine (1998) 'The Nordic States and the European Unity' in Katzenstein, Peter J. (ed.) *Cornell Studies in Political Economy*, London: Cornell University Press

Ingebritsen, Christine and Larson, Susan (1997) 'Interest and Identity: Finland, Norway and the European Union', *Cooperation and Conflict*, Vol.32, No.2, pp. 207–222

Ingebritsen, Christine (1995) 'Norwegian Political Economy and European Integration: Agricultural Power, Policy Legacies and EU Membership', *Cooperation and Conflict*, Vol.30, No.4, pp. 349–363

Jahn, Detlef and Storsved, Anne-Sofie (1995) 'Legitimacy Through Referendum? The Nearly Successful Domino-Strategy of the EU-Referendums in Austria, Finland, Sweden and Norway', *West European Politics*, Vol.18, No.4, pp.18–37

Jonassen, Christen T. (1983) *Value Systems and Personality in a Western Civilization: Norwegians in Europe and America*, Columbus: Ohio State University Press

Kautto, Mikko et al. (ed.s) (1999) *Nordic Social Policy – Changing Welfare States –*, London and New York: Routledge

Keohane, Robert O. (1993) 'Sovereignty, Interdependence and International Institutions' in Miller, Linda B. and Smith, Michael J. (eds.) *Ideas and Ideals*, Boulder: San Francisco: Oxford: Westview Press

Kiel, Anne Kohen (1993) (ed.) *Continuity and Change – Aspects of Contemporary Norway –*, Oslo: Scandinavian University Press

Knudsen, Olav F. (1990) 'Norway: Domestically Driven Foreign Policy' in Heisler, Martin O. (ed.) *The Annals of the American Academy of Political and Social Science 'The Nordic Region: Changing Perspectives in International Relations'*, Newbury Park: London: New Delhi: Sage Publications

Lawler, Peter (1997) 'Scandinavian Exceptionalism and European Union', *Journal of Common Market Studies*, Vol.35, No.4, pp.565–591
Lindal, Sigurdur (1981) 'Early Democratic Traditions in the Nordic Countries' in Allardt, E., Andren, N., Friis, E.J., Gislason, G.P., Nilson, S.S., Valen, H., Wendt, F., Wisti, F. (eds.) *Nordic Democracy*, Copenhagen: Det Danske Selskab
Logan, Donald F. (1992) *The Vikings in History*, London: New York: Routledge
Ludvigsen, Svein (2004) 'Living by the Sea –A National Identity?' (Statement by the Minister of Fisheries and Coastal Affairs in Chicago, 15 October 2004), published 15.10.2004 by the Ministry of Fisheries and Coastal Affairs
Marm, Ingvald (1967) *Norwegian*, New York: Hodder and Stoughton
Mathisen, Stein R. (1996) 'Norwegian Identity and the Whaling Issue' in Anttonen, P.J. (ed.) *Making Europe in Nordic Contexts*, Jyväskylä: NIF Publications
Matlary, Janne Haaland (1993) 'And Never the Twain Shall Meet?', in Tiilikainen, T. and Petersen, I.D. (eds.) *The Nordic Countries and the EC*, Copenhagen: Copenhagen Political Studies Press
McAllister, Richard (1997) *From EC to EU – An Historical and Political Survey* –, London: New York: Routledge
McFarlane, James Walter (1960) *Ibsen and the Temper of Norwegian Literature*, Oxford University Press: London
Mead, W.R. (1981) *A Historical Geography of Scandinavia*, Academic Press: London
Midgaard, John (1963) *A Brief History of Norway*, Oslo: Johan Grundt Tanum Forlag
Miles, Lee (2005) 'The North' in Mouritzen, Hans and Wivel, Anders (ed.s) *The Geopolitics of Euro-Atlantic Integration*, London, New York: Routledge
Miles, Lee (1996) (ed.) *The European Union and the Nordic Countries*, London and New York: Routledge
Miljan, Toivo (1977) *The Reluctant Europeans – The Attitudes of the Nordic Countries Towards European Integration –*, London: C.Hurst&Co.
Mykland, Knut (1996) 'The 17th of May: A Historical Date and A Day of National Celebrations', Source: http://www.cyberclip.com/Katrine/NorwayInfo/Articles/17mai.html, accessed on April 20, 2010.
Nelsen, Brent (1993) *Norway and the EC: The Political Economy of Integration*, Westport, Conn.: Praeger
Neumann, Iver B. (2002) 'This Little Piggy Stayed at Home – Why Norway is not a Member of the EU?' in Hansen, Lene and Waever, Ole (eds.) *European Integration and National Identity: The Challenge of the Nordic States*, London: Routledge

Neumann, Iver B. (2000) 'State and Nation in the Nineteenth Century: Recent Research on the Norwegian Case', *Scandinavian Journal of History*, Vol.25, No.3, pp. 239–260

Nygaard, Kristen (1995) 'Lecture on Norway and the EU', Source: http://www.neitileu.no, accessed on October 04, 2002.

Olson, William Clinton (1991) (ed.) *The Theory and Practice of International Relations*, New Jersey: Prentice-Hall, Inc.

Patomäki, Heikki (2000) 'Beyond Nordic Nostalgia: Envisaging a Social/Democratic System of Global Governance', *Cooperation and Conflict*, Vol.35, No.2, pp. 115–154

Pesonen, P., Todal Jenssen, A. and Gilljam, M. (1998) (eds.) *To Join or Not to Join: Three Nordic Referendums on Membership in the European Union*, Oslo: Scandinavian University Press

Pharo, Helga (1993) 'Norway and the World Since 1945' in Cohen Kiel, Anne (ed.) *Continuity and Change – Aspects of Contemporary Norway*, Oslo: Scandinavian University Press

Preston, Christopher (1997a) *Enlargement and Integration in the European Union*, London: New York: Routledge

Preston, Christopher (1997b) 'EFTA, the EU and the EEA' in Redmond, John (ed.) *The 1995 Enlargement of the European Union*, Aldershot: Burlington: Singapore: Sydney: Ashgate

Punch, Keith F. (2005) *Introduction to Social Research – Quantitative and Qualitative Approaches –*, London: Sage Publications

Redmond, John and Rosenthal, Glenda G. (1998) (eds.) *The Expanding EU – Past, Present, Future –*, Lynne Rienner Publications

Redmond, John (1997) (ed.) *The 1995 Enlargement of the European Union*, Aldershot: Burlington: Singapore: Sydney: Ashgate

Rokkan, Stein (1981) 'The Growth and Structuring of Mass Politics' in Allardt, E., Andren, N., Friis, E.J., Gislason, G.P., Nilson, S.S., Valen, H., Wendt, F., Wisti, F. (eds.) *Nordic Democracy*, Copenhagen: Det Danske Selskab

Rokkan, Stein (1967) 'Geography, Religion, and Social Class: Crosscutting Cleavages in Norwegian Politics', in Lipset, Seymour M. (ed.) *Party Systems and Voter Alignments: Cross-National Perspectives*, Free Press

Rokkan, Stein (1966) 'Norway: Numerical Democracy and Corporate Pluralism' in Dahl, Robert A. (ed.) *Political Opposition in Western Democracies*, Yale University Press

Saeter, Martin (1996) 'Norway and the European Union – Domestic Debate versus External Reality' in Miles, Lee (ed.) *The European Union and the Nordic Countries*, London: New York: Routledge

Saglie, Jo (2000) 'Values, Perceptions and European Integration – The Case of the Norwegian 1994 Referendum –', *European Union Politics*, Vol.1, No.2, pp. 227–249

Sawyer, Peter (1997) *The Oxford Illustrated History of the Vikings*, Oxford University Press

Schechter, Dorothy (1997) 'Edvard Grieg (1843–1907)' in Brown, Berit (ed.) *Nordic Experiences –Exploration of Scandinavian Cultures*, Westport, Connecticut, London: Greenwood Press

Schlesinger, Philip R. (1995) *Europeanisation and the Media: National Identity and the Public Sphere*, Oslo: ARENA Working Paper, No.7

Sciarini, Pascal and Listhaug, Ola (1997) 'Single Cases or a Unique Pair? The Swiss and Norwegian 'No' to Europe', *Journal of Common Market Studies*, Vol.35, No.3, September 1997, pp. 407–433

Scott, F.D. (1980) *Scandinavia*, Harvard University Press: Cambridge, Massachusetts and London

Seierstad, Dag (1997) Conference Paper 'Norway and the EU', Source: http://www.neitileu.no; accessed on October 04, 2002.

Simensen, Jarle (2000) 'National and Transnational History –The National Determinant in Norwegian Historiography' in Frank Meyer and Jan Eivind Myhre (ed.s) *Nordic Historiography in the 20th Century*, Oslo: University of Oslo

Smith, Anthony D. (1999) *Myths and Memories of the Nation*, Oxford University Press

Smith, Anthony D. and Hutchinson, John (1994) (ed.) *Nationalism*, Oxford University Press

Smith, Anthony D. (1992) 'National Identity and the Idea of European Unity', *International Affairs*, Vol.68, No.1, 1992, pp. 55–76

Smith, Anthony D. (1991) *National Identity*, Penguin Books

Smith, Dan and Østerud, Øyvind (1995) *Nation-State, Nationalism and Political Identity*, Oslo: ARENA Working Paper, No.3

Sogner, Ingrid and Archer, Clive (1995) 'Norway and Europe: 1972 and Now', *Journal of Common Market Studies*, Vol.33, No.3, September 1995, pp. 389–409

Sondermann, Fred A. (1991) 'The Theory of the National Interest' in Olson, W.C. (ed.) *The Theory and Practice of International Relations*, New Jersey: Prentice-Hall, Inc.

Sverdrup, Ulf I. (2000) 'Norway: An Adaptive Non-Member' in *Ambiguity and Adaptation: Europeanization of Administrative Institutions as Loosely Coupled Processes*, Oslo: ARENA Report, No. 8

Sverdrup, Ulf I. and Kux, S. (1997) *Balancing Effectiveness and Legitimacy in European Integration: The Norwegian and Swiss Case*, Oslo: ARENA Working Paper, No. 31

Tiilikainen, Teija and Petersen, Ib Damgaard (1993) (eds.) *The Nordic Countries and the EC*, Copenhagen: Copenhagen Political Studies Press

Wallis, Diana (2002) *Forgotten Enlargement – Future EU Relations With Iceland, Norway and Switzerland –*, London: Centre for Reform

Wæver, Ole (2002) 'Identity, Communities and Foreign Policy: Discourse Analysis as Foreign Policy Theory' in Wæver, Ole and Hansen, Lene (ed.s) *European Integration and National Identity*, London: New York: Routledge

Wæver, Ole (1992) 'Nordic Nostalgia: Northern Europe After the Cold War', *International Affairs*, Vol.68, No.1, pp. 77–102

Wintle, Michael (1996) (ed.) *Culture and Identity in Europe*, Aldershot: Brookfield USA: Singapore: Sydney: Ashgate

Wodak, Ruth, de Cillia, Rudolf, Reisigl, Martin and Liebhart, Karin (1999) (ed.s) *The Discursive Construction of National Identity*, Edinburgh: Edinburgh University Press

Primary Sources

Moland, Oddvin (2002) Seminar on 'Norwegian Foreign Policy 1905–2002' at the University of Oslo within the series of 'Norwegian Life and Society Seminars' on October 7, 2002

Hille, Jochen (2002) Seminar on 'Norwegian and Swiss Eurosceptics' at the Institute for Social Research in Oslo on October 29, 2002

Langeland, Nils Rune (2002) (Researcher – Institute for Social Research) Interview on the 'Norwegian History, Foreign Policy and Identity' at the Institute for Social Research in Oslo on November 6, 2002

Marcussen, Martin (2007) (Professor – Department of Politics, University of Copenhagen) Interview on the 'Perceptions, Discourses and Actions of the Norwegian Political Elites' and 'Downloading Europe in the Norwegian Context' at the University of Copenhagen on May 28, 2007

Vallersnes, Finn Martin (2008) (Member of Parliament – Conservative Party, Storting) Interview on 'Norway's Relations with the EU' on May 30, 2008

Kvistad, John Mikal (2008) (Assistant Director General – Section for European Policy, Ministry of Foreign Affairs) Interview on 'Norwegian European Policy' on September 19, 2008